PREFACE

THERE are thousands of amateurs growing orchids in this country, and each year more flower lovers take up this delightful hobby. For generations it has been thought that orchids could be grown only in greenhouses, and backyard greenhouses have sprung up by the hundreds. But in recent years daring folk here and there have experimented with orchids as house plants. Some have succeeded wonderfully, some moderately so, and some have become discouraged with their results. We, ourselves, have been experimenting with various kinds and under various conditions and have lured friends and acquaintances into trying plants in their windows. We have visited home growers in various parts of the country and have corresponded with many more. The evidence now stands definitely in favor of orchids as house plants—not all orchids for every situation, nor just any kind of orchid in any window, but orchids carefully chosen with regard to fulfilling their requirements.

Varying degrees of success or lack of success among those who have tried orchids have led to conflicting ideas on the subject, some of which you may have heard. A discouraging statement may come from someone who has not had good luck with his window-sill orchids. Perhaps his troubles were the result of growing sun-loving kinds in a dark climate, or kinds that need cool temperatures in a warm room, or in not understanding the needs of the plants. An overly optimistic opinion has been circulated by some who evidently were fortunate in the choice of plants for their location and who therefore assume that anyone can grow any kind of orchid anywhere. There are others who have a more realistic approach, who have learned that one kind will do well where another will not, and who have tried various types until they found kinds that would thrive in their particular situations.

We hope in this book to answer many of the questions and eliminate many of the problems that face the amateur orchid grower, to give you an understanding of the plants so as to help you choose kinds suitable for your location, and to help you learn to care for them. We shall introduce you to many different kinds that have been tried in the home and some of their relatives that would be well worth trying. For those who have a greenhouse we shall describe some others that can be grown along with other kinds of plants. We shall try to tell you enough about various kinds to form a background on which to expand your own growing through the years.

I am very grateful to Mr. Donald Wiest of Laramie for the excellent drawings he has made to illustrate this book.

REBECCA T. NORTHEN

Laramie, Wyoming
July 5, 1955

CONTENTS

CHAPTER | | PAGE

I Orchids as House Plants   1

II Orchid Plants and Their Needs   8

III Cattleyas   17

IV Hybrids   26

V Culture of Mature Cattleyas   33

VI Intermediate Orchids—Companions for Cattleyas   45

VII Warm Orchids   59

VIII Cool Orchids   72

IX Potting Mature Plants   79

X Care of Seedlings   94

XI Ailments and Problems   103

XII Artificial Light and Outdoor Growing   112

Index   118

CHAPTER I

ORCHIDS AS HOUSE PLANTS

G ARDENERS want plants in the home as well as outdoors, and even those who own a greenhouse find that plants are still a necessity in the house. Orchid growers are not an exception, and we are typical examples ourselves. We had orchids in the house for more than a year before we had our first greenhouse. Our interest expanded so rapidly that soon we had to have a second greenhouse. Whenever something particularly pretty or interesting would flower we would bring it in the house to enjoy, returning it to the greenhouse when it finished blooming. But that was not enough. We found that even with the greenhouses, we wanted to grow some plants in the house, partly out of curiosity to see what kinds would do well, partly just to have some orchids with us all the time. At present (March) we have seven kinds flowering in two south windows, Cattleya, Phalaenopsis, Dendrobium, Oncidium, Pleurothallis, Maxillaria, and Sigmatostalix. The first four are showy kinds; the last three are miniatures. The Cattleyas are on one window sill; the rest are in a large glass case, a window-size indoor greenhouse, in another window. The case is a yard long and two feet wide, space enough to give growing room to a delightful variety of plants.

Growing orchids in the home is an art slightly different from growing them in a greenhouse. Even those who already have orchids in a greenhouse will find that unexpected little problems arise when they are moved to the house. It is true that orchids will do their best under good greenhouse conditions, and that they are easier to care for in the greenhouse. (The same is true of most of our usual house plants, but we are happy with what they do for us in the home.) Orchids in the home are a challenge, a challenge which

FIG. 1–1. Orchids need a bright window in a home, with several hours of sunlight each day.

makes them an exciting venture, and which makes success with them especially thrilling. It takes ingenuity to meet their demands for good light, to find ways to give some kinds extra humidity, to find a spot for one that needs cooler nights, or another that needs good light but burns easily. Some kinds will grow on a window sill, but others need the protection of a case. Those who cannot have a greenhouse, perhaps because they are not permanently located or because they live in an apartment, would rather have a few orchids and work out the problems than have none at all. Let me quote what two of the many indoor growers have said. A Massachusetts amateur* says, "Window-sill growers have problems which are special. But they also have faith which is pretty special, too, and an undying interest in growing orchids which won't be put off until each and every one of us can have a green-house." A Virginia grower † who has over a hundred plants in four home-made cases and several windows says, "A workable system of home growing takes patience and study, and that alone makes orchids a good hobby."

Orchids are fascinating because of their tremendous variety of sizes, colors, shapes and habits, and their variety of fragrances. There are twenty thousand species, and a mere listing of the hybrids fills several large volumes. Most widely grown by amateurs and commercial growers alike are the more showy corsage orchids, some of which are suitable for the house. The familiar Cattleyas top the list, of course, because of their large size and handsome ruffled lip and because they may be had in bloom at any time of the year. Its hybrids now offer yellow, bronze, and red-violet, as well as the usual lavender and white. The flowers last for ten days, sometimes for several weeks. Phalaenopsis, the moth orchid, has sprays of large, round, flat pink or white flowers that last on the plant from two to five months, longer as a rule than any other flower I know. Cypripedium, called the ladyslipper because of its pouch-shaped lip, is another long-lasting flower, which looks as if it were carved from wax. It comes usually in greens, yellows, and browns, with spots or stripes of red or purple. A fourth popular corsage orchid is the Cymbidium, which does not lend itself to house culture but which can be grown in a greenhouse that runs at 50°F at night. Its waxy flowers grow on tall, graceful spikes, in shades of yellow, chartreuse, pink, green, brown, and white. Many other kinds are grown for corsages in lesser quantities, and some of these are limited to short seasons. Most orchids last well when cut, so that the only limit to their use in corsages is the imagination of the maker and the kinds available. Even those few that do not keep well enough to be of commercial value make stunning and unusual corsages for an evening.

Some orchids have large, bold flowers, while others give tiny fairy-like flowers. Some are incredibly fantastic, some are almost humorous, and some are serenely beautiful. There are miniature plants from one to three or four inches tall, some of which give flowers out of all proportion to the size of the plant, and others that have flowers almost microscopic in size. Orchid plants, whether of miniature or ordinary size, are almost as varied as the flowers in form and habit.

* Paul Stone; *American Orchid Society Bulletin;* January, 1953.
† L. W. Ribble, *American Orchid Society Bulletin;* July, 1953.

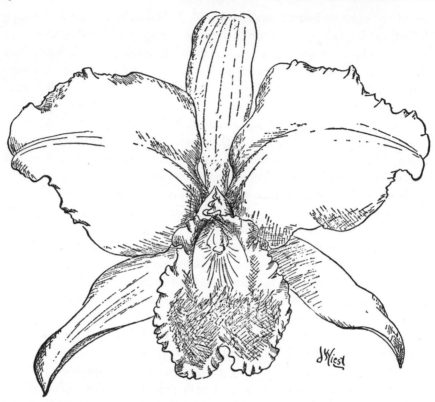

FIG. 1–2. A Cattleya flower shows the basic orchid pattern. The three slender parts are the sepals; the two broader parts to left and right, the petals; and the larger lower part, the lip. Within the lip can be seen the column.

As different as orchid flowers are in shape, size, and color, they are all built on the same basic pattern. The flowers are next above the iris in the evolutionary scale, having come up from lilylike ancestors to become the most highly specialized flowers in the plant kingdom. Like the lily, they are built with three sepals and three petals. The sepals are the outermost flower parts, which serve as the covering of the bud, and which form the background for the rest of the flower. In the Cattleya, and in fact in most kinds, the sepals are more slender and more plain in shape than the petals. Of the three petals in the orchid, one has become so modified that we no longer call it a petal. Instead, it is called the lip, or labellum. The specialization of the lip is one of the modifications that place the orchid high in the evolutionary scale. Nature has done fantastic things with the lip. It is often much larger, more ruffled, more showy, more highly colored than the other flower parts.

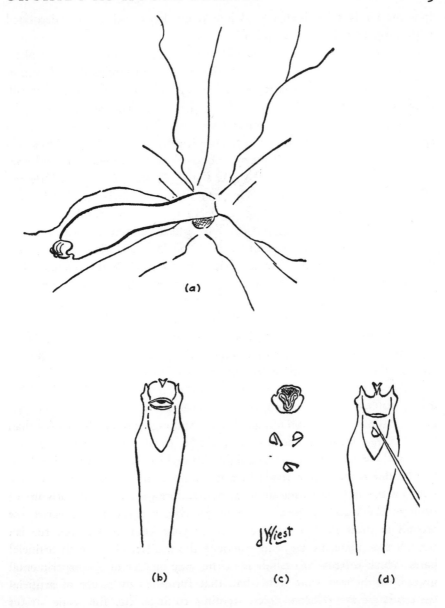

(a)

(b)   (c)   (d)

FIG. 1–3. (a) The column contains the fused anther and stigma, and projects from the center of the flower. The sepals, petals, and lip are attached at its base. Detail of the column: (b) the under side of the column showing the anther at its top and below it the stigma; (c) the anther separated from the column and its pollinia removed; (d) the column with one of the pollinia being placed on the stigma to perform pollination.

In some kinds it has been carved into many lobes and is often decorated with horns or tails, crests or teeth.

In an orchid flower you do not find separate stamens surrounding a pistil. Instead, you find a single, fleshy, club-shaped structure called the column, in which the male and female reproductive parts are fused together. The column is the hallmark of the orchid, another specialization that gives the orchid its distinction in the evolutionary scale. No matter how strange in appearance a flower may be, or how little it resembles anything with which you are familiar, if you find the reproductive organs fused into a column, you can know you have an orchid. At the tip of the column is a little cap which houses the pollen masses. The pollen grains are held together by wax to form hard pellets, called pollinia. There may be two, four, or eight of them. Below the cap is a shiny depression, and if you touch it with a match stick you will find that it contains a thick, sticky fluid. This is the stigma, the receptive part of the female organ, which receives the pollinia. The "stem" of the orchid flower is actually the ovary, which develops into the seed pod after pollination.

Orchids fall into three general groups as far as temperature requirements are concerned—"cool," "intermediate," and "warm"—and this must always be considered in choosing kinds to grow. The largest numbers come in the "intermediate" group, and the requirements of this and the "warm" group are easier to fulfill in a home than those of the "cool" group. No orchid likes a hot, stuffy, or steamy atmosphere, not even the members of the "warm" group. All must have fresh air, good light, and nights somewhat cooler than the days. No orchid, if it is to flower, can be grown on the mantle or on a piano or bookshelf away from the light. An orchid plant, even if it is a kind that would require some shade in a greenhouse, in a home must be in a window. If you have a wide sunny window, through which several hours of sunlight can reach the plants each bright day, you can find a variety of orchids to grow in it. If your climate or your location does not furnish enough sun, there are ways to augment the available light with artificial light. Artificial light for orchids is in the very infancy of the experimental state. Orchids need more light than that furnished by setups of artificial light suitable for African violets, rooting cuttings, etc. But some strides have been made, and contributions can be made by interested amateurs.

The question of the expense of orchid plants usually worries a prospective grower. You have probably read of fabulous prices having been paid for single plants. This is true only of extremely rare ones, or of plants that have some quality of exceptional value to an orchid hybridist. The average cost of orchid plants is about the same as the cost of many potted flowering plants—an Easter lily, for instance. Many charming and desirable species and many inexpensive hybrids can be had for from $5.00 to $10.00. The prices go up from there, but we do not advise paying more for plants until you learn to grow them, and until you know what kinds you particularly desire. When you have learned the habits of mature plants, you can try some seedlings. Seedlings offer an opportunity to acquire fine hybrids without a large initial cost, a subject we shall take up further on.

It is best to buy plants from dependable orchid growers, rather than from dealers who offer spectacular "bargains," or who offer to start you in a business that will soon make you rich. Mature Cattleyas at $1.00 a plant are not bargains because their quality is as low as their price, nor has anyone ever supported himself with the income from a few plants. You can tell the dependable growers from others by the fact that they make no extravagant claims in their advertisements.

You would enjoy belonging to an accredited orchid society and subscribing to a good orchid publication. In most large cities there is an orchid society, just as there is a rose or a lily society. It is a lot of fun to meet other orchid growers, to discuss mutual problems and successes, and to find out what other people are doing. They will welcome you whether you have one plant or a thousand. Many of the local societies are affiliated with the American Orchid Society, Inc., which is international in scope, and many in the West are also affiliated with the Orchid Digest Corporation of California. Both of these organizations publish excellent monthly magazines, in which you will find worth-while articles on many kinds of orchids, cultural methods, new research, the activities of amateurs, news about orchid clubs, and help with problems. Your library probably has copies of these publications, but if not, it would be well worth your while to obtain a single copy of The American Orchid Society Bulletin ($1.00), and The Orchid Digest ($.85). They form the best guide as to where to buy plants and equipment, for the leading orchid growers and dealers in supplies advertise in their pages. Their addresses are: The American Orchid Society, Inc., Botanical Museum of Harvard University, Cambridge 38, Massachusetts; and The Orchid Digest Corporation, P. O. Box 66, Sharp Park, California. If any of the growers are near you it would be well to visit them and to buy plants directly. Otherwise, send for their catalogs.

CHAPTER II

ORCHID PLANTS AND THEIR NEEDS

O<small>RCHIDS</small> grow wild all over the world. They can be found in our own woods and valleys, and even up to 10,000 feet elevation in the Rocky Mountains. The largest numbers grow in the tropics and sub-tropics, where they have a mild and fairly even temperature the year around, and the ones we cultivate in home and greenhouse come from these regions. Yet even in the tropics there is a considerable variety of climate. Some orchids grow in the high Andes, where they are constantly cool and are even covered by frost at night. Many grow in the rain forests at altitudes from 3000 to 6000 feet, where the temperatures stay close to 70°F; others at elevations on down to sea level at progressively warmer temperatures, often exposed to hot sun and drying winds. Some dwell where the air is only moderately humid; some in very moist places such as on cliffs overhanging rushing streams or on rocky coasts where they are washed by salt spray, or in the Pacific Islands where heavy rainfall is the rule. The variety of natural conditions leads, of course, to a variety of habits, and you can readily see that orchids cannot be expected to conform to any one set of rules in cultivation.

Orchids are independent green plants, which make their own sugar by photosynthesis and obtain their mineral nutrients from decaying humus material. They are not parasites.

FIG. 2–2. An orchid plant (Vanda) illustrating monopodial growth habit. It has one main stem that grows taller and adds more leaves at its tip year after year. Side branches may come from the main stem, and these also continue growth from their tips. Flower stems are produced from leaf axils along the stem, as are aerial roots.

epiphytes. Even the terrestrials, which natively grow in the ground, need a more porous medium than our other house plants because they come from the light fluffy medium of leaf mold and rotten wood offered by the forest floor. After many trials and errors, it was found that osmunda fiber, the roots of the osmunda fern, was an excellent medium. Its fibers are tough so that no matter how tightly it is compressed it still allows good air circulation. It is a dead plant material, and as it slowly decays it gives the plants the necessary minerals. Its fibers hold water, and if watered carefully furnish the roots a contact with a damp medium. Growers are still looking for other potting materials. Some have been found for certain kinds of plants that work as well as (some think better than) osmunda fiber. But nothing has been found that is fundamentally better for almost any kind of orchid than osmunda fiber (or osmundine as it is often called). It is easy to obtain, costs around two to three dollars for a gunny sack full, enough to pot a good many plants, and furnishes all the needs of the plants.

Although most orchids have a fairly wide range of tolerance to day temperatures, night temperatures are critical. We shall emphasize the night temperatures for each kind we discuss. Your success with whatever kinds you decide to try will be better insured if you are careful about the night temperatures. A kind that will grow and flower with a night temperature of 55° to 60°F may not flower if kept at 65° at night. Another that will flower when grown with a night temperature of 50° will not flower when the nights are allowed to run above that. The "intermediate" and "warm" orchids comprise a tremendous variety of kinds, whose night temperature requirements of 55° to 60° and 60° to 65° can be met in the home better than those of the "cool" group. But even in this range 5° makes a difference—often between flowers and no flowers, thrifty growth and poor growth.

Some years ago it was thought that all orchids must be kept well shaded, and greenhouses in which they were grown were dark by comparison with greenhouses in which other kinds of plants were raised. Within the last two decades it has been found that orchids do better with much more light than was once allowed them. They make more thrifty, sturdy growth, better root systems, and more flowers of better color and substance.

Light is necessary to make sugar. Sugar is not only the energy food of plants, but the start in the long line of chemicals manufactured by the plant. Fractions of the sugar molecule are combined with minerals from the growing medium to make proteins, pigments, hormones, enzymes, perfumes, etc. A plant that does not have enough light to enable it to make a supply of sugar to meet all these demands cannot grow and flower satisfactorily. It may make only vegetative growth, or if it flowers, the flowers may be of poor quality. We are content with ivy and philodendron, schefflera and sansevieria for their foliage alone. But if we know that a plant can flower in the home we are not happy unless it does so. Furnishing orchids with good light is one of the most vital factors in growing them sucessfully.

Humidity is a problem each grower more or less has to work out for himself, and we shall make suggestions for the individual kinds. We have found that plants in the home seem to need a somewhat lesser relative humidity than in a greenhouse. This may be due to the fact that they receive less strong light in the home, or that there is not such a wide range between day and night temperatures, or possibly that the air in the house is more still than it is at times in a greenhouse, such as when the ventilators are open on a warm day. Whatever the answer, we feel that many indoor growers worry too much about humidity for their plants, and often overdo it. Unhealthy conditions can arise from keeping the plants in a nearly saturated atmosphere. An orchid case, or a Pliofilm or Plexiglas partial case protects the plants from drying air currents and allows a higher humidity to build up. Some kinds do not need this extra protection, and an occasional mist spray over the foliage usually will make up for the low humidity of the house. Whenever orchids are grown in an enclosed volume of air, careful ventilation is necessary. It is better in general to let the humidity rise and fall at intervals than to keep it at a constant level.

The cycle of growth and flowering is about the same for most orchids. They make their new growth during the spring and summer, when the days are increasing in length. Some get a head start by beginning new growth in January, whereas others do not start new growth until May or June, but almost all orchids are showing swelling "eyes" or well-started young growths by March. New root activity accompanies the new growth. Some kinds will flower on the new growths in the summer, others during the fall and winter, and still others wait to flower in the spring. Hybrids, which have been made by crossing various of the species, may inherit the flowering season of one or another of their ancestors, or some may make new growth and flower at any time of the year.

Most orchids have some period during their year's cycle when they appear to be inactive. We do not like to think of this as actual inactivity, but rather as lessened activity. It is sometimes called a rest period. It is a time when the plant is not visibly accomplishing anything; when it is neither making vegetative growth nor producing flowers. However, changes are going on in the plant in preparation for activity to come, and these changes, though too subtle for us to see, are important ones. During the period of lessened activity the leaves are still making sugar, the roots are absorbing water and minerals and the internal cells are manufacturing the various chemicals necessary to the working of the plant.

For the most part the time of lessened activity comes during the autumn or winter, after flowering and before new growth is started, or in some cases between the maturation of the growth and the start of the flower buds. Old-time growers used to "dry off" the plants at this time, giving them scarcely any water at all. We do not feel that such drastic treatment is necessary or beneficial. During late fall and winter, the shorter days naturally cut down the amount of food the plant can make, and cooler temperatures slow down their use of food. Cool temperature also causes the plants to lose water through the leaves less rapidly and reduces the speed of drying of the fiber in the pots. The plants naturally need less water, and we therefore water them less often.

Whether a plant is a species or a hybrid it is its own habits that dictate its care. Always we try to give a plant what it itself needs in the way of water, light, and temperature, and to match our handling to the changing seasons.

Cattleyas are so widely grown that their culture has come to be used as a standard for many kinds and for comparison in the culture of other kinds. It is generally assumed that anyone who grows orchids will have a few Cattleyas. Usually, it is the first kind an amateur desires to own. If you learn to handle Cattleyas, to pot them and water them properly, you can modify the treatment for other kinds. In the following chapters we will first take up Cattleyas and will discuss many of the principles of good orchid culture. Then for other kinds we will say "do not pot as hard as for Cattleyas," or, "water more frequently than Cattleyas," or, "this kind requires about half as much light as Cattleyas." If you should be among the few who do not plan to grow any Cattleyas, we suggest you read this section for the information it contains. Cattleya conditions are typical of the environment needed by the large group of "intermediate" orchids.

CHAPTER III

CATTLEYAS

THE discovery of Cattleyas was an accident, a fortunate happening that gave the world something new, and from which developed a far-reaching interest. The story goes that a Mr. Swainson, in 1818, was collecting mosses and lichens in the rain forests of Brazil. He gathered some heavy, flat-leaved plants to tie around his bundles. When these arrived in England, a Mr. William Cattley, an amateur plant enthusiast, saw the strange plants and took them home with him. In 1824 they flowered, and their magnificent blooms created a sensation in the horticultural world. They were turned over to Dr. Lindley, a renowned botanist, for identification. He found that they were orchids, but of a kind that had not been seen before, and he named a new genus to receive them. The new genus he called *Cattleya,* after the man who rescued them from oblivion, and he gave the species name *labiata* to this first member to be identified, descriptive of its most distinctive feature, its large ruffled lip.

This phenomenon of the plant world sent collectors hurrying to South America in search of more. Oddly enough, it was many years before any other plants of *Cattleya labiata* were found. Other species of Cattleya were discovered in Brazil, Colombia, Venezuela, Costa Rica, among them many that were similar to *Cattleya labiata* and equally lovely. Other orchids new to the eyes of man were also brought back, for which still more genera had to be created. It was truly an era of orchid discovery. Finally in 1891 a tremendous number of *Cattleya labiata* were found, so many that commercial

florists of the day saw in them the possibility that we have seen come true—
that the Cattleya would become the foremost of all flowers for corsage use.

Cattleya labiata is still today one of the most desirable of the Cattleya
species, both for growing and for use in hybridization. It is a radiant rosy-
lavender, has a crisp, waxy substance, and an aristocratic posture on its stem.
Its sepals are slightly pointed, its lip modest in size with a deep purple outer
lobe bordered with lavender and a yellow or cream colored throat streaked
with purple. It flowers from late September into November.

The Cattleyas that are similar to *C. labiata* are referred to as the "labiata
group." The differences are so slight that some botanists would prefer to call
them varieties of *C. labiata* rather than distinct species. However, they are
generally treated as species, and are given as such in catalogs and hybrid
registration lists. The members of the labiata group that are best known
and with which you are likely to come in contact follow. *Cattleya Trianaei*
(Colombia) is somewhat lighter in color than *C. labiata* and has broader
parts and a larger, more round lip. It flowers in mid-winter. Individual plants
may flower for Christmas, but the majority of them come on in January. A
species more dependable for Christmas is *C. Percivaliana* (Venezuela), which
is no longer grown commercially because of its small size, but which is
richly colored and of interest to the collector. *C. Mossiae* (Venezuela) is
often called the Easter orchid because of its spring flowering season. It varies
in coloring from pale blush to rich rose and has a lip veined and mottled
with purple. In some the veining is sparse and not too attractive; in others
so dense that the lip appears to be of almost a solid color. As *C. Mossiae*
finishes flowering *C. Mendelii* comes into bloom, pale blush, sometimes
almost white, with a patch of amethyst at the lower end of the lip. In June
C. gigas (also named *C. Warscewiczii*) flowers, the most showy of all the
Cattleya species. Its lip is very large in proportion to the rest of the flower,
brilliant red-violet set off by two yellow eyes at the opening to the throat.
There are true white forms of each of the above species. One other that is
seldom seen in collections but which has been used in hybridization is the
yellow *C. Dowiana* (Costa Rica and Colombia). The flower shown in Fig.
1-2 is typical of the "labiata group."

There is a less well-known group of Cattleyas, whose flowers are almost
as different from the labiata group as the Cattleyas themselves are from
many other kinds of orchids. These are sometimes called the bifoliate group
because their pseudobulbs bear two (sometimes three) leaves instead of the
single leaf typical of the labiata group. Many have tall, slender, jointed
pseudobulbs. Brown, yellow, green, and various spotted combinations are

found among the flowers, and many are very striking. One is *Cattleya bicolor,* which is green at first, becoming brownish-green after a few days. Its lip is a little red tongue that hangs down from under the column and has no side lobes at all. Another is *C. Skinneri,* which gives clusters of seven to twelve small flowers of a vibrant rosy purple; and somewhat similar to it, though a heavier plant, is *C. Bowringiana* an especially good one for the home. *C. granulosa* has a large green or yellow green flower which has the texture of the imitation orchids carved from wood pulp. The lip of *C. granulosa* has a distinct outer lobe and side lobes that stand up beside the column. It is always fun to have one or two from this bifoliate group because they make such a contrast to the more familiar labiata group.

FIG. 3–1. *Cattleya bicolor,* a green-brown flower with red lip. One of the bifoliate species.

There is some variation among the members of any one species. Some are quite choice, others average, and some of poor shape, color, or size. The best of them rank with the better hybrids, and it is these that have been used to make the hybrids. It is difficult to obtain these choice specimens, because they have been selected out of hundreds of thousands of plants imported from the jungles and are owned by collectors and hybridists. Importation of the species was carried on on a large scale up to about twenty years ago, before there were so many hybrids grown in this country. Now very few wild Cattleyas are brought in. Instead the species are propagated by division, and hybrids will one day replace most of these. During the intervening years the species have been culled, commercial growers retaining the average ones for their cut flower crops. An average-quality species Cattleya should sell for between $5.00 and $10.00. It is difficult for any grower to throw away plants that grow and flower. There is always a demand for the cheap plants and consequently the less desirable ones have frequently been sold to bargain hunters. Many dealers now realize that it is better to destroy the poor plants, for in the end even those who pay very little for a plant are not happy with it. However, there are still large blocks of these plants circulating under the guise of "bargains." At present, if you order a species Cattleya from a reputable grower, you should receive a good healthy plant that will give good flowers.

We enjoy the species because they are the "type" kinds, whose characteristics are appealing in themselves, and form a background to understanding the hybrids made from them. The species described above make good window-sill plants, with the exception of C. *gigas* which is more light-demanding and really requires a greenhouse. C. *Mossiae* is perhaps the best of the Cattleyas for indoor growing, for it seems to be able to grow and flower willingly under a variety of conditions. C. *Trianaei* and C. *labiata* follow as close seconds in ease of culture, and C. *Bowringiana* is rewarding with its wealth of small bright flowers.

The growth and flowering cycle of Cattleya species is typical of many kinds of orchids. The various phases can be followed in the accompanying drawing (Figure 3-2). In late winter or early spring a bud, or "eye," at the base of the latest growth will swell and start to grow. The new growth, called the new lead, extends out horizontally for an inch or so and then curves upward. The horizontal section becomes an extension of the rhizome, while the upward growing portion will produce the new pseudobulb and leaf, and subsequently the flowers. The developing growth is covered with clasping sheathing leaves which later on will dry to the texture of tissue

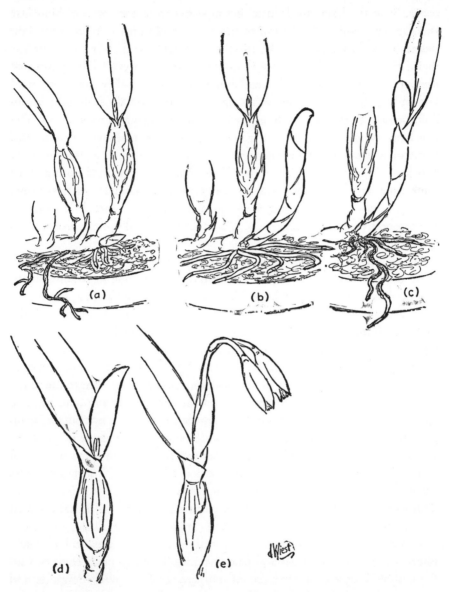

FIG. 3–2. Growth cycle of a Cattleya. (a) A bud at the base of the lead begins to grow. At the same time new roots are formed from the base of the same lead, and old roots make new branches. (b) The new growth lengthens and curves upward, covered by thin sheathing leaves that later become dry. The true leaf is just emerging. (c) The leaf and flower sheath are fully formed. (d) The pseudobulb becomes plump as it matures. Flower buds develop in the sheath. (e) Flower buds ready to open.

paper. Soon the large, thick, true leaf emerges from the last sheathing leaf and rapidly expands. As the leaf opens, down within it can be seen a small, closed green envelope, the sheath, that protects the flower buds during their development. The developing growth and sheath exude honey in thick droplets. While the leaf and pseudobulb are growing, they are tender and soft and can be easily broken. After they reach full size the leaf and pseudobulb become thick and tough, a process called hardening or maturing. The development of the complete growth takes from three to five months. Sometimes two buds will break from the same pseudobulb, giving the plant two leads instead of one, and often buds that have remained dormant for some time at the base of older pseudobulbs will suddenly start to grow. Through the years a plant may develop many leads, and each lead increases the prospective number of flowers. Plants that habitually make many leads are very desirable.

The flower buds develop on a stem from the top of the pseudobulb and grow upward within the sheath. There may be from one to six buds, with two or three the average number. Their progress is slow at first, but as the buds become larger they grow more rapidly. They reach the tip of the sheath in from four to six weeks and then break through the sheath, grow rapidly larger and in about two weeks more are ready to open. The developing buds are green up to this point—pure green for white flowers, tinged slightly with purple pigment in lavender ones. As they prepare to open, the sepals lose the green coloring and take on the color the flower is to be. The opening flower is pale at first and the flower somewhat limp, but as it unfolds the color intensifies and the substance becomes heavier. It takes at the very least two full days to bring a flower to perfection; in some individual plants, four or five days. During the period of maturing the flower parts expand somewhat so that the flower when it is ready to cut is slightly larger than when it started to open. A flower must not be cut until it has attained its full color and substance. White flowers must have lost all tinge of green or cream. If a bloom is cut too soon, it will never acquire good color or substance, but will remain limp and pale and fade after two or three days. Cattleyas should keep in water at room temperature for a week or more, and longer under refrigeration, in water, at about 45°F. The flowers last longer on the plant, two weeks at least, and up to six weeks for individuals of exceptional substance.

Cattleya blooms are usually fragrant while they remain on the plant. Drops of honey are formed by glands at the tips of the sepals and at their juncture with the stem. The fragrance does not last long after the flowers are cut, however, so that to those who have known them only in the florist shop the fact that they are fragrant comes as a surprise.

A wave of root activity accompanies either the flush of new growth each season or the starting of flower buds. One pattern in Cattleyas, which is found in many other kinds, is for new roots to form just as a new lead is starting. Another pattern is for new roots to start just as the flower buds begin to develop. The roots become evident as little bumps on the under side of the basal curve of the pseudobulb. Soon the green tips of the roots break through the dry covering tissues. As the root grows longer, the surface behind the green growing tip becomes white with the developing velamen. The roots are extremely brittle and are easily broken, and they are also tempting to slugs. Injury of the growing tip causes the root to stop growing in length. A root that has grown to about five or six inches in length will form branch roots if its growing tip is injured, and older roots will branch in successive years.

In the accompanying drawing (Figure 3-2) the development of new roots can be followed along with the developing growth. In Figure 3-3(a) new roots are forming along with the starting flower buds; (b) is included to show still a third pattern, illustrated by an Oncidium, in which new roots form from the young growth itself when it is about one-fourth or one-third along. Once in a while a Cattleya growth will form roots when partially developed.

An orchid plant does not have nearly as extensive a root system as our garden plants. The roots are rather thick, and, even though an old plant may appear to have a tremendous number of roots, the total absorptive surface cannot compare to the root system of other kinds, which have thousands of fibrous feeder roots and millions of root hairs. The epiphytic orchids do not have root hairs. The relatively scanty root system must be well cared for if the plant is to thrive, and this creates the great need for caution in watering and for the insurance of good aeration and drainage.

Cattleya species have certain little idiosyncracies in the timing of the various phases of their growth and flowering cycle. Knowing what to expect of a plant helps in caring for it through the year. The patterns shown by the kinds we describe here will also show up in the hybrids, so that a brief summary will not only be of value in growing the species but in pointing out what general kinds of habits to watch for in hybrids, for instance the habit of holding its green sheath for many months before flowering, or of making roots along with flower buds instead of with new growth, or the habit of the sheath to dry before buds appear in it.

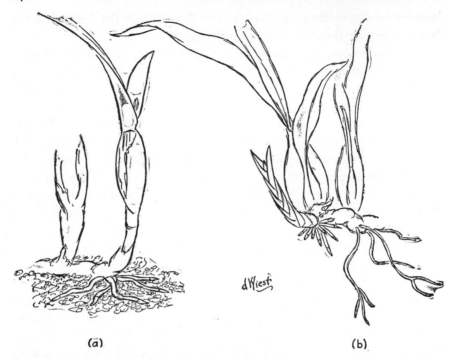

(a)   (b)

FIG. 3–3. (a) Some Cattleyas form new roots at the time flower buds develop, rather than when new growth starts. (b) Another habit of root formation, shown by many kinds other than Cattleya, illustrated here by an Oncidium. Roots form from the new growth as it develops, rather than from the mature growth.

C. gigas goes through the cycle more rapidly than any other. It starts growth in January and develops it rapidly. Flower buds start pushing up in the sheath almost before it has fully emerged from the leaf, and without any pause for the maturation of the growth. The flowers open in June or July. After flowering, new roots form.

C. labiata starts its new growth and new roots together in January or February, and these are well along by March, with the growth mature by July. Flower buds start up in the sheath in early September and the flowers open in October or November. The sheath is double, a sheath within a sheath, and this characteristic shows up in the hybrids. However, other kinds occasionally produce a double sheath even when there is no *C. labiata* in their makeup.

C. Trianaei starts its new growth in March and matures in about August or September. Then, just as the flower buds start up in the sheath in

November it produces its new roots. The flowers open in about January, depending on the habit of the individual plant.

C. Mossiae spreads its complete cycle a bit by having a late spring flowering time. It starts new growth in May or June, not long after flowering. The growth does not mature until about October. Now the plant waits for some months before any further activity is evident. Growers who do not know this habit often become impatient, thinking the plant will never give flowers, and the habit shows up in many hybrids. Then in January or February new roots form, and soon thereafter the flower buds start up in the sheath, to open in April or May. *C. Mendelii* follows this same pattern.

C. Skinneri makes its new roots along with new growth starting in about April. Its growths are mature by the end of the summer, and during the autumn the sheaths turn brown and become quite dry. Flower buds form in the dry sheaths in the winter, sometime during January or February, and open in about two months.

Cypripediums. The giants are not to be worn, but to be shown proudly in exhibitions, to be coveted by admirers, to be enjoyed for the spectacular things they are. Size alone is not of as much importance as quality, however. The average Cattleya hybrid of six to seven inches in diameter retains the grace and charm lost by some of the larger blooms and is a more thoroughly usable flower.

Orchid breeding is not limited to the large types, however. There is a growing interest in smaller flowers such as Dendrobiums, Vandas, Oncidiums, Epidendrums, and many others, partly out of pure delight in their lovely forms and graceful sprays, partly out of the desire for variety in size as well as in kind.

In all hybridization vigor and free-flowering habits are sought. Once upon a time, anything and everything were crossed just out of curiosity, with not much thought to the habits of the plants. Now we realize the value of having thrifty, sturdy plants that give many flowers. A breeder will not use for a parent a plant that is inherently weak or which flowers only occasionally.

There is a very strict system followed in naming orchid hybrids. When two plants are crossed, the grower who makes the cross gives it a name and registers the cross and the name. Every seedling from the cross bears the name of the cross, and if the cross is repeated by anyone else at some other time, the same name must again be used. *Cattleya Mossiae* $\times$ *C. gigas* was named Cattleya Enid, and if you or I were to cross our own plants of *C. Mossiae* and *C. gigas* the offspring would also be called C. Enid. Similarly, *C. Trianaei* $\times$ *C. gigas* was named C. Ballantineana. A cross between two hybrids is named in the same way, for instance, C. Enid $\times$ C. Ballantineana was named C. Bessie Baldwin. Every member of the cross carries this name and, again, the same name must be used for any repetition of this cross. The privilege of naming a cross goes to the person who originates it. Rare cases do come up where the grower fails to name and register a cross, and later on someone who has bought some of the plants may wish to do so. It is necessary then to obtain permission from both the originator and the registration board. Information about registration can be had through the American Orchid Society, Inc.

In buying plants remember that all of the members of a cross travel under the same name, the good and the bad together. When you see a hybrid priced in a list for $35.00, and farther along in the list another plant of the same name offered for $7.00, you can know that the more expensive one is of better quality. Also, if you see a fine plant on exhibition and later order another of that same cross you will probably not get one of equal quality.

Since all the seedlings from a cross bear the same name, a varietal name is used to distinguish an outstanding plant from its lesser sisters. The varietal name is given by the owner, and if the plant becomes famous as an award winner or as a stud plant, its name may become widely known. One of the most famous varieties is Cymbidium Alexanderi, Westonbirt variety, which has been extensively used as a parent. There is as yet no official registration of varietal names. Registration of a hybrid cross is merely a statement of fact. Registration of varietal names would involve a tremendous amount of bookkeeping because often many plants in a cross are given such names, and there is the further question of quality involved. A grower may name plants after all his nieces and nephews if he wishes, according to his own preferences, and a list of registered varietal names would probably include many plants that are not actually worth recording. The owner of an outstanding plant should be most careful to keep all divisions properly labeled.

The only way to increase an individual variety is by division. Self-pollination will lead to a re-sorting of inherited characters. Remaking the cross from which it came might not again produce a plant identical to it, since it itself was purely a chance combination of factors which probably would not come together again in the same way.

Young seedlings are quite inexpensive. You can buy a flask for from $25.00 to $35.00, depending on the number of plants, which may run from 50 to 100. We do not suggest buying a flask unless you have or expect to have a greenhouse. The fifty little plants when put into community pots will not take up much room and can be accommodated in an orchid case, but soon they will need individual pots, and before you know it they will overrun your space. A community pot containing ten or so plants is a good buy, unless you do not want quite that many of one cross. They cost something less than $1.00 a plant usually, a total of about what you would pay for one mature plant. Somewhat older seedlings in two- or three-inch pots are perhaps the best size for most beginners to try, at around $2.00 to $3.00 each. Seedlings about ready to flower range from $10.00 to $25.00 a plant, depending on the quality shown by the first ones that flower out of the cross. If the quality of these first ones is good it indicates that more of those to come may also be good. Still, you take a chance on any individual plant you buy. One may be good, but another bad. Most of us cannot afford to buy very many expensive plants. We feel that the best way to obtain good hybrids is to buy the younger, less expensive plants, for out of several of one cross the chance of having one or two turn out well is better than the chance of having one single plant be a good one.

Intergeneric crosses produce greater variety than crosses made within a single genus, and breeders have long been interested in experimenting with mating closely related genera. The Cattleya tribe contains a number of genera that intercross easily with Cattleya, and untold hundreds of such hybrids have been made.

Laelia is a genus very much like Cattleya in plant form and flower characteristics. The flowers are in general smaller, but have a heavy substance, greater fragrance, a great range of color, and often more flowers to a stem. A cross between Laelia and Cattleya is called Laeliocattleya, abbreviated to Lc. for convenience. Many lovely hybrids are Laeliocattleyas, including most of the yellows.

Brassavola is another genus related to Cattleya, but only one member, *Brassavola Digbyana* has contributed to our modern hybrids. Its greenish white flowers have a tremendous lip, fringed around the edge. The bold shape and size of this lip are handed down in the Brassocattleyas (abbr. Bc.) combined with the richer coloring of the Cattleyas. The fringe may or may not be present in the descendants. The Brassocattleyas have a characteristic fragrance, reminiscent of a combination of citrus fruit oils. Brassocattleya crossed with Laelia gives Brassolaeliocattleya (abbr. Blc.)

The genus Sophronitis contains a member that has bright red flowers, *Sophronitis grandiflora*. The plant and flowers are very small, and it is not frequently seen in collections. We are indebted to this species for much of the reddish coloring in certain hybrids. For the most part it gives only a modification of the purple of the Cattleyas, producing various tones from soft rose to red-violet, and emerges as a definite red only after careful breeding and selection. Sophrocattleyas have been crossed with Laeliocattleyas to produce Sophrolaeliocattleyas, abbreviated to Slc.

The combination of all four genera has been made a number of times, although not very many of these hybrids are well known. In this case, a new name, Potinara, has been applied to take the place of the awkward Brassosophrolaeliocattleya!

So many Cattleya hybrids are available that we hesitate to name even a few. (For a complete list of all hybrids in all genera, from the time of the first hybrid registered to the present day, see Sanders' *Complete List of Orchid Hybrids,* 1947, available through the American Orchid Society, Inc. Two addenda have been published, bringing the list up through 1951.) For every hybrid we name below, there are hundreds of others available, and

before the year is out many more will be registered. The following list gives
a few suggestions, with their color and flowering season. You will notice
that some are primary crosses, crosses between two species, while others
are crosses between hybrids. The parents, given in parentheses, are also
desirable kinds, and dealers will be able to suggest many more.

White

C. Ann Alberts (C. Souvenir de Louis Sander × C. Edithae), winter
C. Bow Bells (C. Edithae × C. Suzanne Hye), fall
C. Joyce Hannington (C. Barbara Dane × C. Snowdon), fall
C. Estelle, alba (C. Cowaniae, var. Enchantress × C. Edithae), winter and
   spring
C. Fay Bainter (C. Ella Mae Sutton × C. Bobby Jewell), any time of the
   year

White with Purple Lip

Lc. Snowdrift (Lc. Cynthia × C. Annette, alba), fall
Lc. Florence Pickard (Lc. Jane Dane, alba × Lc. Brittania, alba), fall
C. Prince John, alba * (C. Hardyana, alba × C. Dowiana, aurea), summer
Lc. Canhamiana (*L. purpurata* × *C. Mossiae*), spring
Lc. Schroederae (Lc. Bella, alba × C. Maggie Raphael, alba), fall

Purple

C. Titrianae (C. Tityus × *C. Trianaei*), winter
C. Enid (*C. Mossiae* × *C. gigas*), fall and spring
C. Hardyana (*C. Dowiana* × *C. gigas*), early summer
C. Fabia (*C. Dowiana* × *C. labiata*), fall
C. Dupreana (*C. Warneri* × *C. gigas*), late spring
C. Portia (*C. labiata* × *C. Bowringiana*), fall
C. Stalin (C. Angus × C. Gloriette), fall
Lc. Bonanza (Lc. Cavalese × C. Prospector), fall
Lc. Frank J. Lind (Lc. Helen Wilmer × Lc. Windermere), winter
Lc. Nellie Cohen (Lc. Canhamiana × C. Ballantineana), spring
Bc. Andes (C. Enid × Bc. Imperialis), fall, winter, spring

* The term "alba," which means white, has unfortunately been given a second meaning,
white with purple lip. If a catalog does not explain its usage, inquire before buying.

Yellow

Lc. Sandra Ozella (Lc. S. J. Bracey × *C. Dowiana,* aurea), summer
Blc. Chief Joseph (Bc. Durga × Lc. Mrs. Medo), summer
Lc. Golden Charm (Lc. Orange Blossom × L. Coronet), winter
Blc. Jane Helton (Blc. Xanthea × Blc. Dorothy Drury Lowe), fall

Greenish Yellow

Bc. Mrs. J. Leeman (*Brassavola Digbyana* × *C. Dowiana*), winter to spring
C. Iris (*C. bicolor* × *C. Dowiana*), fall

CHAPTER V

CULTURE OF MATURE
CATTLEYAS

THE ranks of indoor growers are divided as to whether Cattleyas should be grown in an orchid case or without one. Actually a more important problem is whether the plants will receive enough light. They will do better in a fairly dry situation with good light, than in a humid condition without good light. Most homes are more dry than a greenhouse, and, feeling this lack to be serious, many indoor growers keep their plants too wet, both as to water in the pot and humidity in the air.

When we first obtained an orchid case we put some mature and nearly mature Cattleyas in it, thinking that they would do better than a group which had already spent a successful year on a window sill. To our surprise, those in the case did not do as well as those that were unprotected. The growths were softer and more slender, and came blind, that is, failed to flower. Studies with a light meter showed that plants in the case received considerably less light than those on the window sill, partly because they were farther back from the window and partly because the light had to come through two thicknessess of glass. The plants in the case had had a higher relative humidity than those in the window, but without enough light to make a good supply of food (sugar), they were unable to make as strong a growth and produce flowers. It would seem from this (and we have seen many other such examples) that, if a case is to be used, it must be given a location with exceptionally good light, or the light must be augmented in some way. Otherwise, Cattleyas will do better to be directly in a window.

Nearly mature seedlings have the same requirements as adult plants as to light, temperature, and so forth, and can be included with them in the following directions. There is no difference in culture between species and hybrids.

WINDOW-SILL CULTURE

Light. Plants in a house cannot have the long hours of light possible in a greenhouse. Therefore, the aim is to give them at least several hours of direct light, with the sun actually shining on the plants. The only danger in direct light is burning. The leaves absorb the light and raise their internal temperature to slightly above the temperature of the surrounding air. This increase of leaf temperature becomes dangerous when it approaches 100°F, and burning can occur when the temperature pushes above that. In hot weather the difference between air temperature and leaf temperature leaves only a slight margin, and the burning point may easily be reached. A leaf burn has at first a scorched look, brownish-yellow and almost blistered, later turning dark brown and then black, and finally drying.

The morning sun is not so likely to build up the temperature to the burning point as is the afternoon sun coming through a west window. In a south window the sun from fall through early spring is not likely to burn the leaves, because air temperatures are lower. In all instances, to tell whether the light is too strong, watch the plants themselves. Feel the leaves when the sun is shining on them. If they feel hot to your touch, draw a piece of cheesecloth or some other thin, wide-mesh material, across the glass for just the short period when the sun is pouring in. This will break the light but still allow the plants to have a generous amount. If the leaves feel just gently warm, not hot, let them have the sun straight. The leaves will be a light shade of green with good light, a dark green with less light. In a greenhouse, too strong light will bleach the leaves to a yellow-green or yellow, but we doubt that plants in a home will receive this much light. However, it is good to know how to interpret leaf color in terms of amount of light, and if your plants should be turning yellow with too strong light, then use the cheesecloth shading during the brightest hours.

In general, plants should be set close enough to the glass to receive the sun as early and as late as it can shine in the window. However, some bay windows become quite hot in warm weather, and then it would be well to let the plants stand back a little toward the room, so as still to have the light, but to be a bit out of the heat.

Some orchid growers are fortunate enough to be able to move their plants from one window to another to take advantage of the best light during different seasons. In one home we know of, the plants are kept in an east window through late spring, summer, and early fall, and when the sun swings to the south in the winter, they are moved to a south window. Thus they have some direct sun all year round and make excellent growth and flowers. In our own home, the orchid case has the preference of exposures; it is kept in a south window for the winter sun and moved to a west window during the summer. Our window-sill Cattleyas, however, for lack of another spot, must stay in a south window all year long, where they receive excellent light from fall through winter, but not as much as we could wish in the summer. In another home, the Cattleyas stand directly between an east and a south window, not only receiving good light winter and summer, but having more hours of good light than they would from a single exposure.

Temperature. In speaking of temperature (and of any other environmental condition) we have to realize that the ideal cannot always be attained. Yet it is of value to know what the ideal is, in order to come as close to it as possible. Cattleyas do their best when they can have a night temperature of between 55° and 60°F, which we call "intermediate" in range. These moderately cool night temperatures allow the best growth to be made. Higher night temperatures tend to deplete the food reserves of the plant, using food that should be saved for flower formation. In a greenhouse, the night temperatures can be controlled for the benefit of the plants, but homes are built and managed for the comfort of their human occupants. In a greenhouse, the temperature drops as the sun goes down. In a home the furnace is not turned down until the occupants go to bed. Also, in a home the temperature does not fall as rapidly as in a greenhouse, and the plants do not have as many cool hours as they do in a greenhouse. However, conditions in general are less rigorous in a home than in a greenhouse—for instance, there are not the extremes of temperature, nor the need for as free ventilation in the summer to offset the long hours of sun heat. With the more equable environment of a home, the plants seem to be able to tolerate night temperature a bit above what is considered ideal. This does not mean that night temperature should be ignored, for Cattleyas will grow and flower more successfully the closer you can come to the ideal conditions. But it does mean that if you cannot furnish a place for them where the temperature drops to 55° to 60°F at night, come as close as you can, and try to keep the temperature under 65°F at night.

The temperature close to the glass is usually a little cooler than out in the room. Hang a thermometer with the plants as a check. In cold weather see that the leaves do not touch the cold glass, and check the air temperature directly around the plants, for it may be that they should be moved back from the cold glass a bit in winter.

Summer day temperatures are tolerated pretty well by Cattleyas, with the cooler mornings and evenings to make up for the hotter hours. In addition to burning, mentioned above, another danger of high temperatures is increased evaporation of water from the leaves. Cattleyas cannot make up extreme water loss as rapidly as garden plants, because absorption by the roots is not fast enough. The leaves do not wilt when dry, but over a long period the leaves and pseudobulbs become thin and somewhat shriveled. It does not pay to pour more water into the pot if the fiber is already damp, although the plants will need more frequent watering in hot weather. A light syringing with a mist sprayer when the leaves are warm from the sun will help to make up for loss of water through evaporation. Not only will the plants absorb some of this water, but evaporation from their surfaces will help to cool them. The plants can be syringed in this way several times a day in hot weather, as long as you are careful not to wet the fiber too much and contribute to over-watering of the pot.

Water. It is difficult to give an absolute schedule for watering Cattleyas. As long as the fiber is damp the roots can absorb water, either from the moist air held between the fibers or from contact with the damp fibers themselves. The fiber dries out more rapidly, of course, in hot weather than in cool weather, and in a dry atmosphere than in a damp atmosphere, and more rapidly in a smaller pot than in a larger one. As the fiber approaches dryness, the pot becomes light in weight. When it is completely dry the fiber becomes very light and crisp. Try to judge when the fiber is *almost* dry, and water the plant then, rather than wait until it becomes crisp.

Soak the pot thoroughly when you water. (Do not chill plants with cold water—make it about room temperature.) Stand the pot in water to the rim in the sink and let it remain until the air bubbles stop rising. Let it drain completely in the sink before returning it to its place in the window. Water must not stand in the saucer under the pot, for this not only keeps the fiber too wet but cuts down aeration. To water Cattleyas as you do other plants, by pouring water into the pot while they stand in their usual place, is dangerous. First, the water runs through the fiber into the saucer, which is bad, and second, the fiber does not become uniformly moistened. In a greenhouse we hold the hose to each pot for a few moments, while the water runs out the bottom and over the sides, flooding it until we know that it is thoroughly wet. You cannot do this with a plant in a window, and so in order to insure soaking it it is best to dunk the pot. While you have it in the sink, rinse off the leaves.

Watering too frequently leads to ill health. Waterlogged fiber cannot hold enough air to supply the needs of the roots. When the air spaces between the root cells become filled with water, the roots die for lack of oxygen and their service to the plant is ended. The leaves will become sickly yellow or yellow-green and watery looking. The plants may fail to flower, or produce flowers of thin substance that soon fade, and growths will become smaller, because the roots are unable to absorb enough minerals. Constantly wet (in contrast to just damp) fiber allows an accumulation of toxic materials from bacteria. If the fiber should become soggy from overwatering, it will take two or three times as long for it to dry out as a potful of fiber in good condition. To overcome the waterlogged condition it should be allowed to become completely dry to the crisp state before any more water is applied and then should be watered less frequently so as not to allow the soggy condition to return. In nature the plants are alternately wet and dry. In cultivation we imitate this by giving them a thorough watering and then letting the pots become almost dry before watering again.

Humidity. There is less agreement on what to do about humidity than about most other phases of indoor culture. We have tried some of the suggested methods for window-sill plants, but find that they contribute little, if any, actual increase in humidity for the plants. One, often used, is to stand the pot on a dish of gravel which is kept wet, and another is to stand the pot on a brick in a pan of water. The small amount of water evaporating from either of these is so quickly dispersed into the air of the room that there is but little increase in humidity for the plants. There is a hazard connected with standing the pots on damp gravel. It is easy to let the water accumulate in the gravel so that the pots actually stand in water. If you wish to try this method, be sure to watch the water level. A third method is to build a deep metal box the entire length of the window, which can be kept about half full of water. Over the water is placed a rack of wood slats or hardware cloth, on which the pots are placed. This can be a help for seedlings or other small plants whose shorter stature brings them closer to the water, but mature Cattleyas are really quite tall, and their foliage stands eighteen inches to two feet high, well up into the region where most of the moisture would be already dispersed into the air of the room.

Instead of any of these, we prefer just to give the plants a mist spray occasionally and to rinse off the leaves when watering. However, if your home or apartment is unusually dry in the winter, you may find that a daily spray will benefit them. They soon dry off, but in the meantime will have absorbed some water to replace that lost through evaporation from the leaves. We feel that they will obtain more water in this manner than by the pan-of-gravel method.

CATTLEYAS IN ORCHID CASES

There are many commercially made orchid cases on the market, and many growers have made their own. The design can vary, and the materials of which they are made, but any case that is to be used for flowering-sized Cattleyas, and indeed for most mature plants, must have certain basic specifications. (See Chapter VII.) First, it must be tall and hold a large volume of air. A low, small case is good for seedlings or the smaller botanical orchids. A mature Cattleya plant, however, especially some of the Laeliocattleyas, can be two and a half feet tall from the bottom of the pot to the tips of the leaves. Many produce tall flowering stems which adds even more height. A case in which the tops of the plants touch the glass top would allow no room for flowers. Extra head room not only allows space for taller plants, but has a very real importance in keeping plants healthy. Orchids do not thrive in saturated air. The larger volume of air enclosed by a larger case does not become saturated as easily as that in a small case and does not invite the growth of molds. In a small, close case the plants and pots soon become sticky with mold.

Second, the case must have adequate ventilation. Some cases have doors that open at each end, either the hinged or sliding panel type. Some have the top hinged to swing upward and a door opening at the back or side. We prefer top and bottom ventilation, which allows the heated air to move up and out. The case we use has perhaps the best arrangement of all. A panel at the top is hinged to open upward, and at the bottom on both ends there is a hinged panel that can be opened. This allows a gentle upward movement of air through the case without having to leave either of the end doors open. The end doors give good access to the case for watering

FIG. 5-1. An extended window, which gives more light for orchids, built out from a regular window. The roof is hinged to open upward and the front sections to swing out from the top. At the right is shown the interior. Plastic curtains can be drawn to keep the humidity in the window at a higher level.

and moving plants. If you build your own case, we suggest that you plan to have the ends or the back hinged for this purpose. It is very difficult to reach down through a top opening without breaking flowers or tipping over plants.

At the bottom of the case there should be a pan for catching and holding water. We prefer an open pan, without gravel, as it is easier to clean, but when a heating cable is used it must be covered by sand or gravel. Moisture in the pan adds somewhat to the humidity in the case.

A means of giving Cattleyas good light and still the benefit of a case has been worked out by some amateurs. A partial case is built, by means of a framework fastened around the window. The back, sides, and top are closed by glass or plastic, leaving the front open to the window. Ventilation is provided by hinged doors, or, if a pliable material is used, by rolling back the top and some other section.

A cross between a case and a greenhouse is an extended window, built in place of a regular window and extending outward, with a glass or plastic top. It opens into the room on the inside and is worked from the room, although it may be closed at will by a curtain, a sliding panel, or a door. Like a greenhouse, it can become extremely hot from sun heat and must have regular greenhouse white shading applied to the glass according to the season. Shading can also be provided by tacking cheesecloth inside to the framework. Even with shading to reduce the heat from the sun the plants will receive more hours of strong light than they can indoors. Ventilation to the outside (a top panel that opens upward and perhaps a side panel that also opens) is a necessity, for there will not be enough circulation back into the room to carry out the heated air. Such a window, exposed on all sides to the elements, may need extra heat in the winter, which may be solved by the use of a heating cable and thermostat.

Light. An orchid case, like a greenhouse, has its own little environments even within its small volume. Plants that stand closest to the window will shade those behind them. A plant that stands up tall, or one that hangs, will have better light and a somewhat more dry atmosphere than a low plant or one that stands in a corner. Plants that have different light requirements can be grown together in the same case (providing they all have the same temperature requirement). Those that need the most light can be placed nearer to the window, or raised on overturned pots to allow them to stand up higher. Plants that need less light can be placed toward the back. They will receive less light simply for being farther from the window, so they should not be hidden behind other plants. Cattleyas can thus be grown with kinds that need less light by giving them the brighter places and putting the others toward the back.

The regulation of light has to be related to temperature. Cattleyas on a window sill, open to the free air of the room, can usually take full sun. But the sun shining into a closed case makes it extremely hot in a short time. It is the heat of the sun that is dangerous. When the case becomes hot it must be ventilated at once, or, rather, it should be ventilated before becoming hot. You soon learn to know the seasons—at which times of year the case heats up, and at what time of day to anticipate it. Then, during the hours of heat, open the top and bottom ventilators, and give the plants a mist spray. Watch to see how the temperature runs, and if it is still above 85°F draw a piece of cheesecloth or other mesh material across the window, to cut out some of the light. Try to remove the shade as soon as the sun slants away from the window to allow the plants good light the rest of the day.

A mirror or aluminum foil can be used to reflect light into the case. One grower covers a heavy piece of cardboard with foil and slips this into the case to reflect light from the window onto the back sides of the plants. Another uses a full-length mirror which happened to be on a door adjacent to the case. By opening the door against the case, the morning sun is reflected into the case long before the sun would shine directly into it. (For means of giving artificial light, see Chapter XII.)

Temperature. The temperature requirements are the same as for plants grown on a window sill. Many cases are equipped with a heating element controlled by a thermostat. This makes it possible to keep an orchid case in a location that cools off considerably at night, such as a bedroom or a glassed-in porch, and may enable you to keep the night temperature down closer to the ideal than is possible in a living room. A thermostat must be checked with a thermometer, for it may not be in perfect adjustment with the actual temperature. Either re-set the thermostat, or make a calibration so that you know how to regulate it. It is better to have the temperature controlled between 55° and 60°F than to allow it to go above 60° or below 55°.

One word of caution. If the heating element is in the form of a coil or strip at one side or end of the case, be sure that the plants next to it do not become too hot. During the season when the heat must be used, it may be necessary to move the plants back from the element, or raise them up or shield them in some way from the heat. A heating cable that runs uniformly through gravel over the bottom of the case will not produce localized hot spots, but if the plants are set directly on the gravel they may become too warm. They should preferably stand on a rack of slats or hardware cloth.

Ventilation and Humidity. These are important phases of running an orchid case. While the case is used primarily to furnish a higher relative humidity than contained in the atmosphere of the home, the plants and the interior of the case must be allowed to dry off at least once a day. Even when temperature conditions do not require opening the ventilators, as described above, they must be opened to allow the air to change. We have found that if the ventilators are kept closed for two or three days in a row the pots and plants surfaces become sticky. Algae and fungi develop in the damp surface of the fiber and on the pots. It is easier to prevent this than it is to get rid of it. A suggestion is to keep a ventilator cracked open during the day and to close the case at night. During the day when the case warms up, it is of course necessary to open the ventilators wider.

It is difficult to name an ideal percentage of relative humidity. Our Wyoming climate is very dry. Ten to fifteen percent relative humidity is about normal, with a rise to 40% when it rains and an occasional drop to 5%. The relative humidity in the closed orchid case usually stands at about 40% from evaporation of water in the pan and from the plants themselves. Just after watering or misting the plants, the humidity will rise to 60% or 70% and will remain so for some time if the case is kept closed. However, while it is good for the plants to have the higher humidity at intervals, we do not like to keep it at this high level for long periods, for in order to do so we must either keep the ventilators closed all the time or wet the plants very frequently. It is better to let the plants be alternately wet and dry; to let the air in the case move out and be replaced with fresher, drier air each day; to syringe the plants while the sun is shining on them, with the ventilators open; and then, in the evening to close the case.

On warm, damp summer evenings it may benefit the plants to open the case and the window next to it to give them all the fresh air they can get. In regions with hot summer nights this may also be a good practice, for in some areas the house just does not cool off as much as could be desired at night.

Watering. The pots in a protected case will not dry out as fast as pots on a window sill, yet still the fiber must approach dryness between waterings. If by some chance the plants should become overwatered, as evidenced by rotting roots or yellowing leaves, or by a sticky, soggy condition of the fiber, let the pots dry out thoroughly to the point of crispness of the fiber.

An individual plant that becomes soggy can be moved out of the case for a week, or even two or three weeks if necessary, until it has dried off. Complete drying will help kill off any molds or algae that have developed in the wet fiber and allow waterlogged roots not yet killed to recover.

FIG. 5–2. Some equipment for the orchid grower. Upper left, a sprayer that gives a fine mist. Upper right, a bulb-type sprayer that gives gentle streams of water, useful especially for syringing hanging plants in a case. Center, two sizes of potting sticks.

Plants in Flower. Ventilation is very important when plants are in flower. It does not hurt the flowers to have an occasional mist spray of water and, in fact, may help maintain their freshness in hot weather. But they must not remain wet for long. In a close, dank atmosphere a fungus may develop on the flowers, causing brown or pinkish spots. Free ventilation will help prevent this. If some flowers should develop spots, they should be cut off and destroyed at once to prevent spread of the fungus. Plants in flower should be watered the same as otherwise, with the usual care not to overwater.

If You Have a Greenhouse. Cattleyas may be grown with a mixed group of plants if the temperatures you maintain are suitable. Often in a greenhouse there are spots where the temperature will run a littler cooler or a little warmer than the general range. By checking with a thermometer you may find a place exactly suited to Cattleyas. Shading must be arranged for the plants.

FEEDING CATTLEYAS

Osmunda fiber provides the minerals essential to growth and flowering. If Cattleyas in osmunda are given the proper conditions of light, water, and temperature, they should perform satisfactorily. However, experimentation has been going on in giving orchids extra minerals in the form of chemical fertilizers dissolved in water, and it has been found that some kinds benefit greatly. Growers are in agreement that Cymbidiums, Phalaenopsis, and Dendrobiums, for instance, do much better when fertilized. Most growers also agree that Cattleyas benefit from fertilizers, but they do not need as much. Also, there is a narrow margin between the amount that benefits and the amount that produces undesirable effects. The temptation to fertilize too frequently or too heavily is hard to resist, and we believe that before using any fertilizer for Cattleyas a beginner should grow his plants for a year to learn their normal habits, and to learn to recognize healthy growth.

Overfeeding of Cattleyas brings a number of bad results. One is the production of soft vegetative growth without flowers. Another is the starting of many leads that do not develop normally. Still another is the accumulation of salts in the fiber, which upsets the normal functioning of the roots. To avoid such troubles it is good practice to give fertilizer not more often than once in two weeks, to flood the pots with plain water in between times, and to fertilize only when the plants are in active growth and when light conditions are good. If you find that the season's growth is soft and blind, or that any of the other conditions arise, it would be wise to carry the plants through the next season without giving them fertilizer.

Minerals can be absorbed by the leaves and stems of plants as well as by the roots. Instead of applying fertilizer to the pot, the solution may be sprayed on the leaves at bi-weekly intervals, so-called foliar feeding.

Wilson's Orchid Fertilizer and Gaviota Orchid Fertilizer, developed especially for orchids, are both good. Hyponex or similar chemical fertilizers may also be used, at one-half the strength recommended for other kinds of plants.

CHAPTER VI

INTERMEDIATE ORCHIDS —
COMPANIONS FOR CATTLEYAS

Tᴴᴱ intermediate group of orchids contains a wide variety of kinds that make good companions for Cattley-
as. Some have little idiosyncracies that may even make them easier to grow
in certain places than Cattleyas. In a greenhouse there may be places that are
warmer or cooler, shadier or sunnier, than the average, which may offer just
the right spot for one or another of these kinds. In a home many of us are
limited to one or two good spots for orchids, but even so a large variety of
kinds can be grown together. There are far too many to be even listed here.
However, we shall describe a number and tell their particular needs, with
suggestions as to where they may best fit in home or greenhouse.

CATTLEYA RELATIVES

The Cattleya relatives include a number of genera, some of which are
frequently crossed with Cattleya as described in the chapter on hybrids.
Actually very few of the hundreds of species have been thus used, and many
are grown for their own appealing qualities as species.

Epidendrum is a genus full of variety, with about a thousand species
that grow from Mexico through tropical South America. One type, of which

45

E. O'Brienianum is an example, has very tall reed-like stems, at the top of which arises a long, slender flower stem bearing a huge cluster of dainty, reddish flowers. When grown out-of-doors they can reach a height of five feet. *E. O'Brienianum* itself is too tall and "leggy" to be particularly attractive as a plant except for warm-climate gardens. For the sake of their lovely, feathery flowers, hybrids have been made from it that have better proportions. These new types make airy, graceful plants of from twelve to eighteen inches in height. They come in colors ranging from yellow through orange to red, and the little flowers hold themselves with the tiny fringed lip uppermost. They make a delightful addition to either greenhouse or home, placed side by side with Cattleyas and grown in the same way.

Perhaps the most handsome of all Epidendrums is *E. atropurpureum*. The plant is about the size of a Cattleya, with pear-shaped pseudobulbs that bear two leaves. The two-foot long sprays of fragrant spring flowers are very showy, with curving brownish green sepals and petals and a bright rose lip. It demands good light and can take a few degrees of warmer night temperature than Cattleyas, but otherwise is handled the same. Once the flower buds are well developed it can be moved to almost any spot and will continue to bloom. Therefore, if there is not room for its flower spray in the place where you grow it, you can move it to a table or mantle and enjoy it there for two months. Cattleyas, also, and in fact all of the kinds in this chapter can be kept out in the room while in flower, being returned to their growing place when they have finished.

Epidendrum prismatocarpum is another plant of Cattleya proportions, handled in the same manner. It has tall spikes of little waxy greenish-white flowers barred and spotted with purple. They lend a striking note in a collection of large flowered kinds.

Two delightful small Epidendrums are *E. fragrans* and *E. cochleatum*, which grow happily with Cattleyas but should be kept a little more damp. Indoors, they should perhaps be in an enclosed window or in a brightly lighted case. *E. fragrans* is white with a candy-striped lip. *E. cochleatum* is greenish in color, and its slender sepals and petals stream down from its upright shell-shaped lip, reminding one of some little marine creature.

A beautiful Epidendrum for an orchid case is *E. difforme,* which likes about half as much light as Cattleyas and a higher humidity. It has slender, jointed stems six to eight inches tall, from the tops of which come clusters of delicate, waxy, greenish-white flowers in midwinter. They are sweetly scented and surprisingly long lasting. This species rapidly grows into a dense cluster of stems that make an attractive little plant.

Epidendrum tampense, a small plant with pseudobulbs only an inch tall and thick, narrow little leaves, is an inexpensive but charming orchid. It is rather widely advertised as the "butterfly" orchid, although the term seems not particularly suited to it, and it is often suggested that it be grown on a small log. We find that it does better in a pot in osmunda, watered frequently enough to keep the fiber damp. It gives delicate sprays of small, reddish-yellow or reddish-green flowers in early summer.

The genus Laelia has many species that come close to Cattleya in appearance. *Laelia autumnalis* and *L. anceps* are pretty and easy to grow. They

FIG. 6–1. *Epidendrum atropurpureum,* a popular and showy species with greenish purple flowers with a rose-colored lip. It is delightfully fragrant.

Fig. 6–2. *Epidendrum difforme,* a delicate and lovely small species, with reed-like stems and waxy, greenish white flowers.

are much alike, with three to five perky, rosy-lavender flowers borne on a tall stem. While the plants are fairly short in stature, the length of the flowering stem may necessitate moving them out of their usual spot while flowering. Their requirements are the same as for Cattleyas, with emphasis on good light.

Two yellow Laelias that make attractive additions to a collection are *L. flava,* pure yellow, and *L. tenebrosa,* a bronze-toned yellow, both of which have been used as parents in the making of yellow Laeliocattleya hybrids. The first flowers in the fall; the second in the spring. They are not much seen in collections, but are available and are well worth trying by those of you whose fancy runs to species and who want something unusual. They like good light but should be given a little extra shade when in flower.

Brassavola, the genus that contributes *B. Digbyana* as a parent of the Brassocattleyas, has another species that is easier to grow and is more readily available. This is the "lady of the night," from Central America, *Brassavola nodosa.* Its small, white flowers pour forth a fragrance in the evening entirely out of keeping with their modest appearance. Its leaves are nearly terete, thick, and almost round like a pencil. The lip is shaped like a pointed spade, and the sepals and petals are slender and spidery. It grows willingly with somewhat less light than Cattleya and seems not to mind if the temperatures run a little cooler or a little warmer than the Cattleya range. It flowers in the fall. It should be watered like a Cattleya.

ONCIDIUM

Words are heavy things to describe the airy, sunny, little figures that pose on the flower stems of Oncidiums. They seem to be tiny dancing creatures dressed in yellow, or yellow and green, or yellow and brown. Oncidiums are native to the same countries that give us Cattleyas, yet there are hundreds of species that range from the warm lower altitudes to the cooler higher places. In a greenhouse you would have room for a larger number, but in an orchid case the number would be limited by their need to receive the best light possible. They should stand next to the window or be suspended from the top of the case.

A famous Oncidium is *O. varicosum, var. Rogersii* whose wide, round lip and abbreviated petals and sepals have earned it the nickname "dancing doll." It is a small plant, only about eight inches tall, yet can give a flower spray three to five feet long, many-branched, with 100 to 250 bright yellow flowers about the size of a quarter or fifty-cent piece. It flowers in the fall after having made its growth during the summer. It should be kept at the cooler end of the Cattleya temperature range during the winter, else it may not do so well the following season. It likes more frequent watering than Cattleyas while growing and flowering, but should become dry between waterings in the winter. It should be in a case or enclosed window during the summer for the extra humidity. Be sure, however, that it gets plenty of light. If its flower spray becomes too large for the case, remove it to a window. It would be best to keep it at 55°F in winter, even if it means removing it from the case, but it must still have good light.

A close rival of *O. varicosum* for flower size and shape is *O. ampliatum,* but its spray is shorter and more compact. It likes the same treatment. Its flat cluster of turtle-like pseudobulbs make it suitable for growing on a slab, to which a chunk of osmunda fiber has first been wired. But if you grow it this way, give it a daily watering and an occasional application of fertilizer.

A number of other well-known Oncidiums can be handled in the same way as these two. *O. splendidum* and *O. Lanceanum* have larger flowers than most, strikingly marked with brown and green. Other familiar Oncidiums are *O. flexuosum, O. Cavendishianum,* and *O. sphacelatum.* A species with dainty pink flowers is *O. ornithorhynchum.*

For an orchid case there are two little Oncidiums that have not been well known, but which are becoming popular. They are available from Panama and can be had through dealers who import species from this area. They are almost miniature plants, four to six inches tall, that come from fairly low altitudes. They are very tolerant of temperature differences and will do well with night temperatures ranging all the way from 55° to 65°F, and although they can take a good bit of light they will also do well with less. They are *O. cabagre* and *O. obryzatum,* which give long slender, branched sprays of little yellow and brown flowers. The stems are flexible and can be looped over a screw near the top of the case, from which place they hang down in a graceful manner. Several plants can be put on a piece of hanging bark or a twisted branch, to which small chunks of osmunda have been wired, giving the effect of a little jungle garden. (See Chapter VII.)

ODONTOGLOSSUM

Many of the Odontoglossums require cool conditions not easy to find in a home, but a few lend themselves to Cattleya conditions. *O. grande,* called variously the "tiger" orchid or the "clown" orchid, has large, waxy boldly marked flowers that last well when cut and make stunning corsages. The sepals and petals are yellow, barred with brown. The lip is white, barred with brown, and at its base is a fat, little rubber doll formed by protuberances from the lip. *O. grande* likes somewhat more frequent watering during its growing and flowering season than Cattleya, but during the winter is allowed to become dry between waterings. Like *Oncidium varicosum,* it should have the cooler end of the Cattleya temperature range during the winter. The flower spikes come from the new growth in late summer, before the growth is mature, and the flowers open in September.

Odontoglossum Schlieperianum is a summer flowering small edition of *O. grande,* with the colors tending a bit to green and orange.

O. citrosmum is quite different from these two in that it bears drooping sprays of delicate pink and violet flowers in the spring.

Fig. 6–3. An almost miniature plant, *Oncidium obryzatum,* that gives a wealth of tiny, long-lasting yellow and brown flowers. The flower details at the right show front and back views.

FIG. 6–4. The "tiger orchid," *Odontoglossum grande,* has bold yellow and brown flowers.

CYPRIPEDIUM

There are Cypripediums for almost all conditions. These are the lady-slipper orchids, native to southern Asia and related to our North American Cypripediums. Actually, their generic name is Paphiopedilum, but they have been called Cypripediums, or just Cyps, for so long that the name clings. They are terrestrial, with no pseudobulbs, but make new growth each year as does a Cattleya. A few of the species are popularly grown, but most of the kinds available are hybrids. Those species with plain green foliage like temperatures a bit cooler than Cattleyas, and those with mottled foliage temperatures a bit warmer. Hybrids between the two suit Cattleya conditions nicely.

The Cypripedium flower is built on the fundamental orchid plan, but at first it may be hard to see this. The lip is pouch-shaped and holds within it the column. The shield-shaped structure standing at the top opening of the lip is a part of the column. Under this structure are two anthers, one on each side, and the pollen is a sticky mass instead of in the form of a hard pellet. Swinging down into the pouch is the tooth like stigma. On each side of the lip, standing out like two arms, are the petals. The large banner-like part that stands at the top of the flower is the dorsal sepal, and the similar part underneath the lip is formed from the fused lateral sepals.

The flowers are often fantastically colored in combinations of green, brown, yellow, red, purple, and white. The dorsal sepal has usually a ground of white or green and is variously spotted or striped with purple, green, or red. The petals and lip are colored in a simpler fashion. The waxy flowers make stunning corsages for either daytime or evening wear.

Cypripediums like about half the amount of light required by Cattleyas. In a greenhouse they should have extra shade, enough to keep the foliage a rich green. They make a good kind for an orchid case where there is good light but not enough for sun-loving kinds. They must not be allowed to become dry in the pot, and they benefit from applications of fertilizer solution according to directions. If they are grown on a window sill they should have the foliage misted once or twice a day. Actually, they will probably do better in the humid air of an orchid case, especially in dry climates. If you wish to grow them in a case along with kinds that demand more light, put the Cyps toward the back away from the brightest sun.

Cypripedium insigne and its larger type, variety *Harefield Hall,* are perhaps the best known and most widely grown of the plain-leaved, or cool, kinds. They are the progenitors of many hybrids. Their flowers are yellow or yellow-green with quite a variation in shape and marking. *Cyp. insigne* will not make flower buds unless it has a night temperature not above 55°F. It can therefore be grown in a cool spot in an intermediate greenhouse or in a home where the night temperature can be maintained at this level during the winter. We also suggest the plain-leaved Cyps for a cool orchid case (see Chapter VIII).

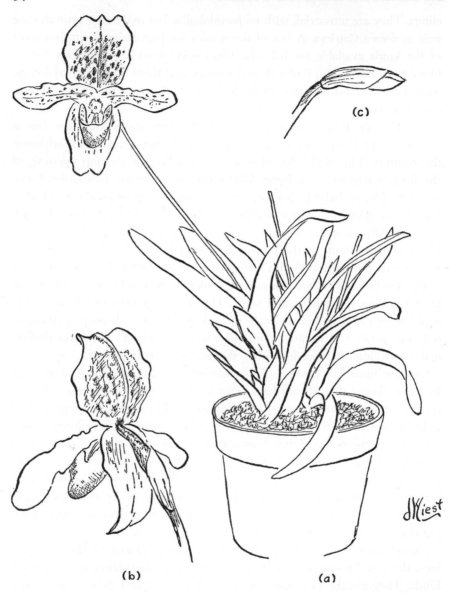

(c)

(b)   (a)

FIG. 6–5. *Cypripedium insigne,* a popular species. (a) Plant in flower, showing new growth coming from its base. (b) View of a flower from the back, showing the large dorsal sepal and below it the fused lateral sepals, the petals standing out to the sides, and the pouch-shaped lip. (c) Flower bud emerging from its sheath at the top of the stem.

Some other species, also frequently used in hybridization, can be grown with a night temperature of 55° to 60°F, among which are *Cyp. niveum, Cyp. Lawrenceanum, Cyp. Argus, Cyp. callosum,* and *Cyp. villosum.* Many hybrids are available and in general are a little easier in their habits, making them better for growing in the home.

Cyps are potted in osmunda that has been chopped fairly fine, giving it a softer texture than that used for Cattleyas. The plant is removed from its old fiber, is set in the new pot, and the osmunda is packed in as firmly as you can manage with your fingers. Some growers have their own special Cyp composts. A plant need not be divided unless the growths in the center part have become old and have lost their leaves. When this happens, the "lines" of growth can be separated to make divisions of three growths each.

STANHOPEA

Stanhopea is one of the strangest of orchids. The flowers look like a cross between an eagle and a squid. The plant must be grown in a basket because the flower stem bores down through the osmunda and comes out the bottom. As the stem lengthens, the buds become large and fat. Then one day they swing out away from each other, and the next time you look the flowers are wide open. Some fortunate growers have seen the sudden opening of the flower and say that it give an audible "pop." The broad sepals arch outward, the petals flare up between them like wings, and the fantastic lip and column hang down like talons of a bird of prey. The lip is armed with a pair of horns at its tip, and above is carved into a contorted central thickened part.

The flowers last but three or four days, but are well worth the year's wait for the spectacular show they give. The pear-shaped pseudobulbs are topped by a single, broad, veined leaf, and the roots are armed with inch-long, sharp, spine-like extensions. Since the basket dries out rapidly, it needs frequent watering. It thrives under Cattleya conditions, with good light, and while it is probably too large for a case would be worth trying in a larger indoor space such as an enclosed porch. Some species of Stanhopea are *tigrina, oculata,* and *Wardii,* all native to Central America.

CYCNOCHES

The Panama "swan" orchid, *Cycnoches chlorochilon,* is one of the loveliest of orchids. In the center of the chartreuse flower sits a white lip, shaped somewhat like the body of a swan, above which curves a long slender column that reminds one of a swan's neck and head. Even if it were not so lovely to look at, its fragrance would endear it to all. As the flower warms up in the morning the perfume fills the air, sweet yet spicy. By evening the fragrance diminishes.

FIG. 6–6. The "swan orchid," *Cycnoches chlorochilon*, loses its leaves as the flowers develop. The chartreuse and white flowers are extremely fragrant.

The pseudobulb bears six or seven broad, satiny, veined leaves. The flower stem arises from one of the top nodes, and as the buds develop the leaves begin to fall. Usually the pseudobulb is naked by the time the flowers open. Cycnoches grows easily at Cattleya temperatures, with a bit less light, making it a good kind for an enclosed window or an orchid case. It should not be allowed to dry out while growing and flowering, but during the winter and until new growth starts should be kept fairly dry. The flowers have a peculiarity worth knowing. The anther at the tip of the column is easily disturbed. At a sharp touch the pollinia spring from their place. A forceful jet of water or bumping the flowers with the hand can do it. A flower will soon fade when this disturbance happens. Only the flower that has the anther loosened is affected. To keep the flowers for their full span of two weeks, treat them gently.

VANDA

Except for a few species, Vandas, in general, like conditions a little warmer than Cattleyas. However, many growers are successful with them by hanging them at the brighter end of the Cattleya house, which gives them not only a little more warmth but the brighter light they need. You would have to have exceptionally good light in order to grow them indoors, and this might be furnished by an extended window or a sun porch. They do best where the night temperature does not go below 58°F.

Vandas are monopodial orchids, as illustrated in Chapter II, and do not have pseudobulbs. They add new leaves to the top of the stem year after year. Branch stems do likewise. They have tremendously heavy aerial roots which cling to the osmunda, the basket, or to anything with which they come in contact. They must have free aeration and for that reason do better in a basket or a slotted pot. Baskets are made from strips of cypress wood or redwood and can be obtained from dealers in supplies. They require a higher humidity than Cattleyas, but a daily mist spray can make up for this where the humidity is not maintained at a high enough level. They thrive with a bi-weekly application of a chemical fertilizer.

They come in a great variety of shapes and colors. The flower spray comes

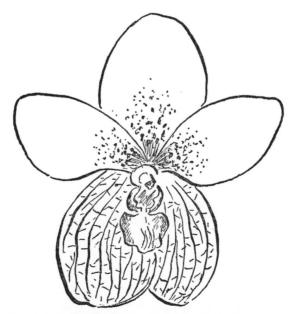

FIG. 6–7. A hybrid that shows its *Vanda Sanderiana* parentage.

from a leaf axil on the younger part of the plant. *Vanda caerulea* is blue and
has given its blue color to many hybrids, such as *V. Rothschildiana* (*V.
caerulea* × *V. Sanderiana*). *V. caerulea* is one of the species that likes a bit
cooler temperatures than the others and may be grown in a cool but bright
spot in a Cattleya house. *V. Sanderiana* is the largest flowered of the species
and a parent of many hybrids. The upper half of the five-inch flower is
pinkish lilac, dotted with red-brown at the base of the petals, while the
lower half is a yellow-green suffused with brown and marked with a network of brown lines. You can usually spot the hybrids that have *V. Sanderiana* in their makeup, for many of them carry this typical network of darker
color. *Vanda teres* has terete leaves (cylindrical) and has lovely, full flowers shaded from white to rose. Hybrids between this and the flat-leaved
kinds (called the strap leaf species) give what are called semi-terete kinds.
Many hybrids are available in an array of colors. We also suggest Vandas
in the following chapter for warm conditions.

CHAPTER VII

WARM ORCHIDS

THE orchid case really comes into its own for humidity-loving warm orchids in the average home, the home where night temperatures are maintained between 60° and 70°F. Certain warm orchids are less of a problem in the matter of light than most intermediate kinds and grow and flower happily where the latter might fail. Many indoor growers who have first tried Cattleyas and their companions without much luck have finally found success with the less light-demanding warm orchids. There is nothing more lovely than a miniature greenhouse in the living room, filled with a fascinating variety of orchids. A Phalaenopsis plant in flower gives a note of beauty for months. A gay little Oncidium literally fills the case with its yellow and brown blooms. A rosy purple Dendrobium adds a touch of rich color. A striking green and white Cypripedium sends its flower up on a tall stem to catch the eye. Miniature orchids and small "botanical" kinds are especially suited to the intimacy of an orchid case.

In our own orchid case we have some twenty-five plants, a veritable bit of the jungle world. There are always flowers. At first we may have to point out the smallest ones to the observer, but because they are so intriguing they sometimes provoke the greatest interest. That number of plants in a volume 36 inches long by 24 inches wide and 42 inches high may sound incredible. Fifteen, however, are miniature plants growing on various hanging perches—a "tree" made of a twisted piece of sagebrush wood, a little raft, a piece of bark; seven are plants that need only three-inch pots and take up little room; and the rest are quite large Phalaenopsis plants. There are ten genera represented, with two or three species in some and a few hybrids in others. Some have grown up in the case from seedling stages and have now flowered for their second and third time.

FIG. 7–1. An orchid case in a living room window. Note the top and bottom ventilators, as well as the end door. The plant in the extreme left corner is a Pleurothallis; next is a young Dendrobium, then several Phalaenopsis, an Oncidium, and a number of miniature orchids on hanging arrangements. A piece of cheesecloth is pulled across the window when the sun is hot.

The orchid case should stand in a window that receives sun part of each day. Since the plants in the back part of the case are farther from the window, they will receive less light, so that the sun should actually shine into the case. Even so, these plants farther from the window will not have as strong a light as those in front. This position can be reserved for those that can do with less, such as seedlings, or a plant actually in flower, or a kind that is a bit more shade-loving, reserving the better light for others. Hanging plants receive better light than those that stand in the bottom of the case in a back corner. The trick of hanging some plants enables you to grow many more than would otherwise be possible. Although the warm orchids like a higher humidity than most intermediate kinds, care must still be taken to protect the plants by ventilation and by shading drawn across the window when the hot sun is shining into the case.

The kinds we suggest here like a relative humidity that fluctuates between 40% and 70%. When we have just watered or sprayed the plants with water, the air reaches the higher relative humidity. Then we let the humidity gradually fall so that there will not be too close an atmosphere. Our climate is normally dry, yet even so we ventilate the case for several hours a day. In a damper climate it might be well to let the ventilator stay open a crack a good bit of the time. The case has a pan in the bottom to catch water, and it usually has water in it. (Incidentally, this must be watched so that it does not overflow.) The plants stand on a rack of redwood slats over the pan. Evaporation from the pan and from the plants themselves keeps the humidity higher than that in the room.

Watering has to be gauged by the plants themselves. They dry out less rapidly than they would on a window sill, but small pots and especially hanging plants will dry out faster than you might think. We would rather water frequently, syringe occasionally, and give good ventilation than keep a high constant humidity. If you should find that the case has been too damp or the pots too wet, it will not hurt the plants to let everything really dry out to clear up the situation. But try not to have this happen very often!

PHALAENOPSIS

These lovely orchids like gentle treatment and gentle conditions. They want no extremes, in the direction of either heat or cold, especially when in bud, but are not as tender as this might indicate. They will do well with one-half or one-third of the light intensity required by Cattleyas, but should have their light for as many hours as the window can allow.

Phalaenopsis is monopodial in growth habit. It has a single stem, from the tip of which one or two new leaves are produced each year. The thick, silvery roots grow from between the leaves and travel into the pot or over its sides to wander along the bench or down between the slats. They remain

Fig. 7–2. A white Phalaenopsis hybrid. The flowers are perhaps the longest lasting among orchids, blooming through most of the winter. An especially good kind for an orchid case and a serenely beautiful orchid.

active for years unless the growing tip is injured. When this happens, the root will send out a branch or two, but the roots do not typically branch as freely as those of Cattleya. Since the plants are slow growing (in contrast to Vanda), a mature plant takes up about the same amount of space year after year. It is said that some may attain a diameter of three feet, but an average plant is about ten inches tall with leaves eight to twelve inches long. The individual leaves remain green on the plant for a number of years so that a plant may have five to ten leaves at a time.

The usual growth pattern is for a new leaf to start in the spring, with new roots showing at the same time. The leaf matures in early fall. Another leaf may start later in the fall when the flower spike appears. The flower spike comes from the base of the plant. Its length and the number of flowers it bears depend on the condition of the plant together with the inheritance of the plant. The first spike on a seedling is likely to be small and to have but four or five flowers. An older plant may have a spike over two feet long with twelve to twenty flowers. Such a long flower spike necessitates raising the plant on a block or overturned pot in order to show off the whole array of flowers.

The flowers are open and flat, with broad, plain sepals and petals. The lip is small, occupying the center of the flower, but is intricate and decorative. The chief colors are white and pink. The white hybrids are the larger flowered and have greater keeping qualities. It is difficult to describe their texture—it is somewhat of the quality of a rose petal, but heavier, almost like doe skin. The sprays consist of single stems with the flowers alternately arranged in perfect symmetry. Sometimes the whole spray may be open at once, but often the buds at the tip are slow to open so that the flowers develop in successive sets. Since individual flowers may last from two to five months, the spray may hold flowers for the better part of a year. Most of the hybrids are superior to the species and are readily available. Some famous hybrids are P. Doris, P. Elizabethae, P. Katherine Siegwart, P. Altadena, to name but a few, and each year new hybrids are produced with these and others as parents.

The pink kinds have typically smaller flowers, but the spray is branched and holds more blooms. The flowers do not keep as long as the white, but longer than many other kinds of orchids. They are largely derived from the species *P. Schilleriana,* which is as lovely as many of the hybrids.

There are a few other types, some with yellow markings, and some rare and odd species. If you should become a collector of Phalaenopsis, you will want to investigate these, but to start with we suggest you obtain the white or pink hybrids.

As has been indicated, Phalaenopsis thrive with a night temperature that ranges between 60° and 70°F at night. We do not like to let the night temperature go to the higher end of the range during the winter, but it is all right in the summer. Day temperatures should be around 72°F in the winter, a little warmer when the sun is shining into the case, but even then not above 80°F if possible. Warmer summer days are unavoidable, but try to keep the temperature moderated by the use of shade, ventilation, and syringing. Extremes in temperature can cause the buds to turn brown and fall off—either sudden chilling, often coupled with dark weather, or too high temperatures by night or day.

Watering depends somewhat on the climate in which they are grown. Some Florida growers say to let them dry out between waterings, while those who live in dry climates prefer to keep the osmunda fiber damp at all times. The relationship between watering and atmospheric conditions is obvious, for what may seem "dry" in Florida would be considered damp in Wyoming. However, the point is to see that the plants have fairly constant moisture at the roots coupled with humid air and good aeration.

Phalaenopsis benefits from an occasional application of liquid fertilizer, such as Wilson's or Gaviota, given according to the directions of the manufacturer.

The plants may be grown in pots or baskets, according to your preference, though it is more difficult to remove them from the latter for repotting. Osmunda fiber is generally used, potted somewhat more loosely than for Cattleyas. The best time to repot is when a new leaf and new roots are starting. The root crown of the plant should stand just above the fiber to assure the best aeration. If you buy plants from Hawaii, they may arrive in baskets filled with chunks of charcoal, or if you visit certain growers in this country you may see them growing in gravel. When grown in gravel or charcoal they must be watered every day. When grown thus, the plants depend entirely on fertilizer for mineral nutrients. If you wish to try either of these methods, use the same fertilizer recommended for plants in osmunda, but alternate the fertilizer with plain water, giving one one day and the other the next.

DENDROBIUM

A dendrobium especially suited to an orchid case is *D. Phalaenopsis* (so named because its flowers resemble Phalaenopsis in shape) and its hybrids. They must be placed to receive the best light available. These are sympodial plants, which make a new pseudobulb each season. The pseudobulbs are slender and jointed, often called "canes," and have leaves at the joints. A young plant may have only four to six leaves on a pseudobulb eight to ten inches tall, but as the plant grows older the pseudobulbs become taller and have more leaves.

FIG. 7–3. *Dendrobium Phalaenopsis* adds a rich note of purple to a group in an orchid case. The growth to the right is flowering for the first time, while that on the left has bloomed twice. Flower details show front and side views.

The flowers are about two and a half inches across, one spray holding five to fifteen flowers. *D. Phalaenopsis* has white sepals tinged with blush, petals of a rosy lavender, and a darker lip. Hybrids and selected strains range from this light coloring through various shades of rosy purple to deep violet, the last of which is still rather rare. The flowers have a short spur at their base, formed by an extension of the column (a "foot") to which the petals and sepals are attached.

New growth starts in early summer and matures in the fall. As the last leaf reaches full size, the flower spike can be seen coming from the tip of the cane. At the same time the canes from the previous year may produce second flower spikes, from the axil of one of the top leaves.

Dendrobiums have a small root system, consisting of rather slender roots. They are usually potted in osmunda fiber, potted as you would a Cattleya, in pots small for the size of the plant. A plant that has three or four canes thrives in a three-inch pot, while a four-inch pot is large enough for a plant of five to eight canes. *D. Phalaenopsis* and its hybrids should be kept moist at all times, with an application of fertilizer solution given every two to four weeks, depending on the kind used.

CYPRIPEDIUM

The mottled leaf Cypripediums and their hybrids, some of which were suggested for growing with Cattleyas, will also do well in an orchid case along with Phalaenopsis. Their need for less light, a humid atmosphere, and temperatures around 60° to 65°F at night make them well worth trying. One that has been frequently grown in cases is Cyp. Maudiae, an old but distinctive hybrid, much loved through the years. It is a cross between *Cyp. callosum* and *Cyp. Lawrenceanum,* with mottled foliage and a striking green and white flower that stands up on a tall stem. For other hybrids for the warm orchid case, we suggest you correspond with growers who specialize in Cypripediums.

SMALL ORCHIDS

There are so many kinds of small orchids that you will find different species listed as favorites, or offered in catalogues, or available from collectors. Some grow natively at fairly low altitudes, shaded by the larger plants around them, and these should do well in an orchid case. Here is a field of exploration for you, to locate such species through collectors. While many of the commerical growers in this country lean toward one or another of the corsage kinds, some import the odd and unusual species and offer them for sale as well. Often they can obtain things for you that they do not regularly stock, and it is better to have their help in importing unless you obtain references for a foreign dealer.

Most of the Oncidiums require brighter light than Phalaenopsis, and some need cooler temperatures. But the two small species mentioned in Chapter VI, *O. cabagre* and *O. obryzatum,* do beautifully in the warm orchid case. The former has tiny bird-shaped flowers of brown with touches of yellow, and the latter little flowers of greenish yellow. The delicate sprays are from eighteen inches to four feet long, but the stem is so flexible that it can be draped where you want it in the case. (The stem of the larger Oncidiums is strong and heavy and cannot be bent without breaking.) Another species to try is *O. ornithorhynchum* (the "bird-beak" orchid), a small plant that gives a dainty spray of little rosy purple flowers.

Bulbophyllum is another genus suited to an orchid case. Plants are available from growers in this country. One of the most popular, in fact a most amazing little plant, is *B. Medusae* (also called *Cirrhopetalum Medusae*), of creeping habit, about six inches tall. Its flowers, cream-color spotted with purple or yellow, grow in dense clusters. The lip and petals are minute, but the tendril-like sepals are several inches long, giving the effect of a tiny Medusa head. The Bulbophyllums should be kept moist while growing and flowering, but should be watered less frequently during the winter. Like Dendrobiums, they should be placed to receive as good light as the case affords.

Plants of Stelis and Pleurothallis are decorative with or without flowers, but their tiny flowers are fascinating. Stelis has little paddle-shaped leaves on slender stems, the whole plant being only two to four inches tall. The dainty flower spike arises from the base of the leaf and is in itself only three or four inches tall, but it bears twenty or more three-pointed flowers. The petals, lip, and column are so reduced in size that they can barely be distinguished with a magnifying glass, while the sepals alone form the conspicuous part of the flower. Some are red, some greenish white; on some the flowers last over a week, on others they open and close in a day. The plants quickly multiply into a lush cluster. One individual in our collection gave sixty-five sprays of flowers last year.

Pleurothallis is a genus in which many plants look like large editions of Stelis, and there is a good bit of variation in height and leaf shape as well as in the flowers. Among the smaller species is one that we consider the prettiest of all orchids as far as foliage is concerned. It is *P. cardiothallis,* which has pointed, heart-shaped leaves borne on slender stems. In the center of each leaf appear the little brownish red flowers, one at a time. As soon

FIG. 7-4. A charming miniature orchid is Stelis, which grows equally well with warm or intermediate kinds.

as one fades, another takes its place, and this goes on for years for each leaf.

Both Pleurothallis and Stelis need to be kept moist at all times, and they will do well with warm orchids, or with the Cattleya group if given a little more shade.

These various little kinds lend themselves to the making of a miniature orchid "tree," or to being grown on a piece of bark or in a small basket. The "tree" is made from a piece of driftwood or wind timber, or any interestingly shaped branch. Chunks of osmunda fiber are wired to the branch and in its crotches with rust-proof wire, and the plants are then wired to these. New roots soon grow into the fiber and through it to anchor the plant to the wood. The "tree" is suspended from a brass screw driven into the upper framework of the case. A piece of rough bark from a fallen tree also makes a natural-looking orchid perch. Osmunda fiber can be forced into the crevices in the bark, or may be wired to it, and plants fastened thereto. Not only do such devices make possible growing more plants in a case by holding them up to the light and out of the way of other plants, but they display these small orchids and their flowers in a charming manner.

A small potted plant may be hung also by loops of wire. In hanging plants in a case, place them at the ends and the back side where they will receive light but will not shade other plants.

The dime store offers refrigerator baskets in various sizes and shapes. They are made of wire covered with plastic so as to resist rust. We have used a number of these to make miniature gardens, each holding four or five small plants. Osmunda fiber is packed into the baskets in chunks, and the little plants are nestled into place by inserting their roots into the space between the chunks, allowing the rhizome or root crown to rest along the groove. If they are not held steadily enough at first, we fasten them to the fiber with a large wire staple.

OTHER USES FOR ORCHID CASES

A doctor who grows orchids added an orchid case to his waiting room, partly out of a desire to have orchids to enjoy in his office, partly for the purpose of decoration. He discovered that the case had an unexpected and appealing effect. The miniature greenhouse with its alluring contents sparked the interest of his patients. He found them fascinated by plants they had never known before so that they were as eager to ask questions about the orchids as to describe their ailments. Patients who came regularly watched with curiosity the development of flower buds. He could

Fig. 7–5. An orchid "tree" made from a twisted branch, with miniature plants fastened to pieces of osmunda wired to it. The dainty sprays of flowers are a small Oncidium. The "tree" is hung by a wire loop in the end of the case.

sense the salutary effect of the orchids on their troubled spirits. Actually, what he had done was to give his patients the same mental and spiritual lift that he himself found among his plants at home. Such a use for an orchid case is a challenge to all amateurs. A possibility that comes to mind is for a group of growers to pool their resources to place an orchid case in a hospital waiting room. Possibly, since personal care of the case would not be feasible, they might contribute plants by the week that are already in flower, replacing them frequently as the flowers fade. Another suggestion for a hospital is to maintain a case in a ward where patients are confined for long periods, or where it could be enjoyed by a group of old folks who not only have to tolerate long confinement but who are often lonely.

VANDA

We discussed Vanda along with intermediate orchids because many can be grown in a warm, bright spot in a Cattleya house. They are also suited, of course, to a warm greenhouse, with night temperatures between 60° and 70°F. Because of their demand for good light we do not suggest them for a case that houses Phalaenopsis, but they might be tried in a brightly lighted case by themselves, or in an extended window or sun porch.

CHAPTER VIII

COOL ORCHIDS

T HE cool orchids comprise a number of lovely kinds, some of which are suited to growing in an orchid case in a room where the winter night temperature drops to 50°F, or can be kept between 50° and 55°F (not over 55°F). You can choose between those that do well with moderate light, about the same as required for Phalaenopsis as described in the previous chapter, and those that must have bright light. Remember, however, that even kinds that are less light demanding deserve the best light you can give them. There is not quite as wide a choice in the cool group as in the intermediate and warm groups. However, for a bright location you will find some in the intermediate group whose temperature requirements overlap the range given here (kinds about which we said "will do well at the cooler end of the Cattleya range") which will grow along with the light-demanding Dendrobiums of the cool group.

The kinds specifically suited to the 50° to 55°F temperature range do not like winter temperatures above this level, but, like most other kinds of orchids, will take warmer summer nights. There is a fourth group which is so intolerant of heat that we might call them "cold" orchids. They require air-conditioned greenhouses in many parts of this country. These are chiefly the high-altitude Odontoglossums, such as *O. crispum* and its hybrids, whose culture is tricky at best and which we will not take up for this reason.

The methods of handling the cool orchids in an orchid case are fundamentally the same as outlined for the other groups: careful ventilation to prevent constant saturation of the air and the building up of heat; shading against the heat of the sun at its peak; and attention to proper night temperatures.

CYPRIPEDIUMS

The plain-leaved Cypripediums, described in Chapter VI as needing a night temperature of 55°F, such as *Cyp. insigne* and its hybrids, are good subjects for the cool case, and many growers do well with them in a cool window. If the lists of dealers do not specify which Cyps are cool growing and which warm, better ask before buying.

MILTONIAS

Miltonias are not as widely grown as Cypripediums, but a number of indoor growers have had success with them, and where cool conditions are possible they are certainly worth trying. They make good companions for the cool Cyps, since their light requirements are about the same. They are botanically related to Odontoglossum and Oncidium, and come from the cool altitudes of the South American rain forests. They are pretty plants, with somewhat flattened pseudobulbs and slender leaves. Their nickname, "pansy orchid," describes the character of their flat, gently rounded flowers, which grow on slender stems arising from the base of the pseudobulb. The flowers are fairly long lasting on the plant but do not keep well when cut.

The chief problem is to keep them cool enough in areas with hot summers. The Cypripediums are more tolerant of summer heat than Miltonias. If you live in a warm climate, we would not advise Miltonias for your first orchids, for they require an experienced hand where conditions are not ideal. In our northern states where the summers, notwithstanding hot spells, are, in general, not extreme they may do very well. They should be shaded sufficiently from the sun at its peak so as not to have great heat, yet they must have enough light to mature their growths well. An east exposure is perhaps best, where they can receive good light during the morning hours before the day becomes hot. They should be given good light through the winter.

Miltonia is grown in this country in the soft, brown osmunda fiber. Some growers pot them every year, in pots large enough to accommodate the year's growth. Other growers pot them every two years. They should be potted when new growth starts in the spring, but do not tolerate being shifted in hot weather. If new growth has not started by April, you have a choice of potting them in anticipation of new growth, or waiting until early fall. It would seem, since our fall weather is often quite warm, that potting in the spring is preferable. About one-third of the pot should be filled with crock for drainage. The fiber should be firm, and some growers like to have it convex on the surface to insure aeration at the base of the plant.

Miltonias should be watered frequently enough to keep the fiber damp, with the usual care not to produce a soggy condition. During their growing season they benefit from applications of fertilizer, as suggested for both Cypripediums and Phalaenopsis.

Some of the well-known species have large, showy flowers, and many hybrids have been made from them. *M. Roezlii* bears two to four large flowers. The sepals and petals are white, the latter tinged with purple at the base, while the large white lip is yellow at the base. This species is a bit more tolerant of warmth than the others and might be worth a try where summers run warm. *M. spectabilis,* which gives one large flower to a stem, is notable for its violet-purple lip set off by blush-colored petals and sepals. *M. vexillaria* bears up to ten flowers to a stem, of a lovely pink color. There are several horticultural varieties of this species that range from yellow to purple.

DENDROBIUM

Again, here is a genus that has members to suit various conditions. *D. nobile,* a kind that requires bright light, can be grown along with intermediate kinds in the summer, but must be put in a cool spot at least during the fall and early winter in order to make flower buds. We keep it with cool orchids all year round, in a greenhouse where it receives really bright light. It is grown successfully by some indoor growers who can give it both good light and cool nights when flowering time comes. *D. Nobile* is what we call a deciduous type. Its pattern is to flower on the growths made the previous year, not on the current season's growths, and these eighteen-month-old growths lose their leaves just before flower buds are made. The two- to three-inch flowers come from the upper nodes of the jointed pseudobulbs, in nodding groups of two or three. They are velvety, with rounded sepals and petals, white tinged with purple, and a round lip that is purple bordered with white. The plants should have generous watering while growing, and two periods of lessened watering, between the completion of growth and formation of flower buds, and between the end of flowering and start of new growth.

Dendrobium Thyrsiflorum and *D. densiflorum* are evergreen types that have four-angled pseudobulbs bearing four or five dark, glossy leaves. The flower sprays arise from the swollen upper nodes and bear an eight- to ten-inch-long, densely rounded cluster of completely charming little flowers. The former has white sepals and petals and a yellow lip, while the latter is all yellow, and both have the rounded lip fringed. They have a sparkling crystalline texture. They are grown with the same temperatures and light conditions as *D. nobile,* but do not have as pronounced rest periods.

ODONTOGLOSSUMS

The Odontoglossums need more sun than the cool Cyps and so are suggested as companions for the Dendrobiums. It could be, however, that a few Odontoglossums and Dendrobiums could occupy the front half of a case, near the source of light, and would serve to break the light for some Cyps and Miltonias. The Odontoglossums given here should be handled pretty much like the Cyps, not being allowed to dry out in the pot, and should have a mist spray over the foliage during the bright hours.

Odonto. bictoniense gives sprays of small yellow-green flowers with a rose-colored lip, and blooms in the fall. *Odonto. pulchellum* is spring flowering, with small sprays of white flowers that smell like lily-of-the-valley. *Odonto. Rossii* gives short sprays of rather large flowers, white marked with dark brown, in winter.

CYMBIDIUMS FOR A GREENHOUSE

The conditions under which Cymbidiums are most easily grown, and under which the average grower will be successful with them, are not necessarily the only conditions under which they may be grown. The ideal conditions come with a naturally cool climate where there is plenty of sunshine all year, and where the plants can have summer nights of under 60°F and winter nights of 50°F. These conditions also fit such crops as carnations, and we suggest that, where carnations can be grown, Cymbidiums should do well. Even where conditions are naturally ideal, not all growers do well with Cymbidiums. On the other hand, some growers have found ways to raise them in climates heretofore considered too hot for Cymbidiums. There have been more failures than successes in warm climates so far, and so we do not feel justified in recommending them at present. Hybridizers are working to devolop kinds that will flower in warm regions, and before too many years there may be more or less standard types and rules of culture for these areas. Nor can we recommend them as house plants because of their demand for exceptionally good light.

If you have a greenhouse in which you can give Cymbidiums cool nights and bright light, you should surely try a plant or two, for they are very handsome orchids. The plants have rounded pseudobulbs about the size of a fist, which bear eight to twelve long, slender leaves. The roots are fleshy and stay within the compost. They are variously called semi-terrestrial and semi-epiphytic. The flower spike arises from the base of the pseudobulb, within the axil of one of the lower leaves, and grows two to three feet tall (sometimes more). It appears in the fall, and the flowers open from December through April, depending on the habit of the particular plant. The flowers are waxy, three to five inches in diameter, in colors ranging from white through shades of yellow, green, brown, pink, and various subtle combinations of these. They keep for several weeks on the plant, and almost as long when cut. Unlike Cattleyas, the flowers will open after the spike has been cut. If a spike is cut when the lower blooms are open and put in water, it can be enjoyed for a long time while the other buds open in turn.

Cymbidiums can be grown in osmunda fiber to which is added some well-rotted cow manure, or in a fibrous compost that allows free aeration. They must be kept well watered at all times, and they benefit from frequent syringing of the foliage in warm, bright weather. The syringing helps to keep under control their chief enemy, red spider (see Chapter XI). They are known as "heavy feeders" and should have a weekly application of chemical fertilizer during their growing season.

Shading has to be adjusted to the season and local conditions. During the summer, although they demand good light, the hot summer days allow the heat to build up too much in the greenhouse. Shading must be applied to the glass, but not so heavily as to deprive them of good light. It must be combined with free ventilation and a fan to keep the air circulating. The ventilators can be left open day and night. Some growers move the plants out of the greenhouse for the summer, either into a lath house or under tall trees. Although Cymbidiums can take an occasional frost without apparent damage, it is wise to move them back into the greenhouse before frost is expected.

As cooler days come on, increase the amount of light gradually. As winter arrives, and flowering begins, shading will have to be adjusted to the locality. In cold climates, where the sun does not build up the heat in the greenhouse so much, less shading is necessary. In climates with mild winters, the flowers will have to be protected from the warm sun. Areas with more or less dull winters will allow Cymbidiums to have clear glass.

New growth starts in late winter or early spring in some kinds, or in late

FIG. 8-1. Cymbidiums are handsome plants that do their best in a greenhouse with cool nights. The tall spike holds many waxy, long-lasting flowers. Insert at left shows a vegetative growth developing, usually distinguished from the tightly pointed flower spike (right insert) by the separating leaf tips.

summer in others. Growths that start early should produce spikes that autumn, but those that start in the summer will not flower until the following year. In the latter types you will see vegetative growths coming shortly before spikes start from the same pseudobulbs.

Cymbidium hybrids are superior to the species and are more easily obtained. We suggest that you consult with growers who specialize in Cymbidiums as to kinds to buy.

CHAPTER IX

POTTING MATURE PLANTS

T HE general method used for potting Cattleyas can be applied to other orchids, with only slight modifications. Where such modifications are necessary, they have been described.

An orchid needs repotting either when it has outgrown its pot, that is, when more than one growth has gone over the edge of the pot, or when the fiber has become broken down. But if the plant is in good health and the fiber is good and firm (not crumbly or not shrunken so that the plant wobbles in it) it may not need repotting for three or four years.

All orchids should be repotted during their period of active root formation, preferably just as the new roots are starting so that they will grow into the fresh fiber. There is no point in repotting a plant at all unless you give it a chance to reestablish itself quickly. Hence we do not advise shifting a plant when its growing season is over and it is not able to make new roots for several months. A plant that is disturbed at such a time is forced to spend a long period without functioning roots and may be set back considerably. In those kinds that form new roots from the newly developing growth, the time to repot is when the growth is two or three inches tall and new roots are expected in a few weeks. In kinds which form new roots from the mature lead at about the time the "eye" begins to swell, the time to repot is just when those new roots are evident as little "bumps" and before they have begun to grow rapidly. When the new roots are lengthening they

79

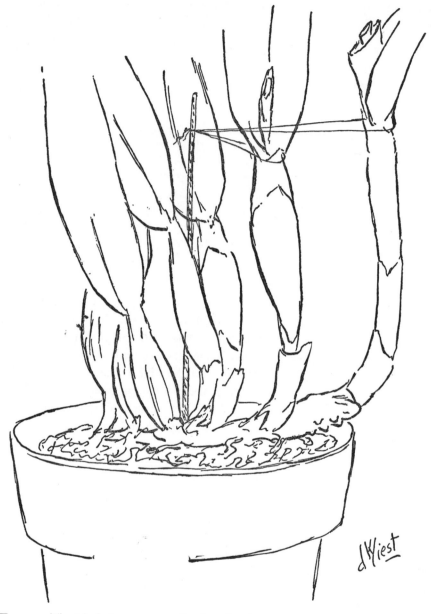

FIG. 9–1. The ideal time to pot a Cattleya is when new roots are evident as little bumps on the under side of the lead.

are easily injured, and so we do not like to handle a plant with the new roots from one-fourth inch to about six inches, of which more information in a moment.

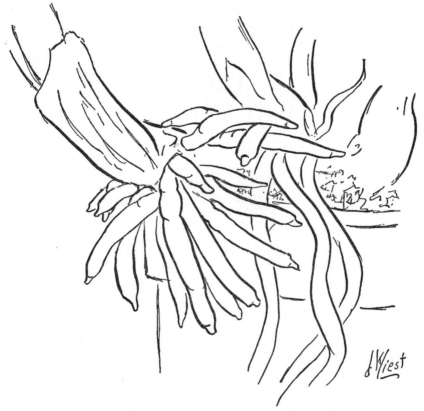

FIG. 9–2. New roots too far along to be handled without injury.

As the new roots start from the lead, the wave of activity spreads to older roots, and these send out many branches. Old roots of which the tips have been injured, even those that look quite brown and dead, will send out new green tips all along their length. They thus assist in making new roots, expanding the root system year after year, and for this reason it pays to take good care of them. When repotting we are careful to leave clean stubs of the old roots, which quickly give rise to branches and, together with the new roots from the lead, furnish a wealth of active roots.

While the old roots branch freely from a short stub, new roots do not seem to have this capacity for some time. If they are injured while still quite short, their activity for that season comes to an end. However, if they are

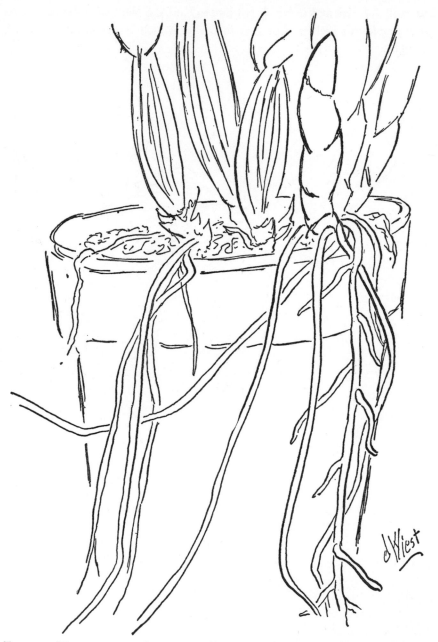

Fig. 9–3. New roots are about six inches long, at which length they branch if the tip is cut off. Plants can be potted at this stage.

allowed to grow until they are six inches or so in length and then should be injured, they will send out branch roots. This gives us a second chance to repot a Cattleya whose new roots get started before we can get the job done. Also, it is handy for plants that make new roots while flowering, for instead of trying to shift them with buds that could be damaged, we can wait until flowering is over.

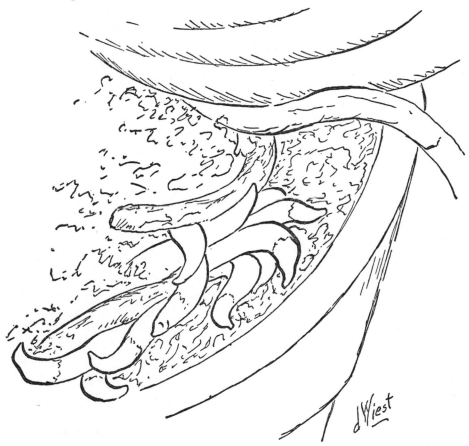

FIG. 9–4. Cut stubs of roots, both old and new, give rise to branch roots that quickly re-establish the plant.

DIVIDING PLANTS

Some growers like to keep plants small, keeping them down to five- and six-inch pots at the most. Commercial growers often do this with their selling stock, for a one-lead plant is priced lower than one with several leads, and this size is easier to pack. They are also more uniform as to space and watering. Other growers, ourselves included, find that a plant with many leads can take less space than the same plant divided into smaller sections. For instance, a plant of five pseudobulbs with a single lead may stretch across a five-inch pot, while a plant with three leads spreading out fanwise would also fit a five-inch pot. A plant in an eight-inch pot can have eight or nine leads and will produce more flowers than the number of single lead plants that could occupy the same space. We move plants on into larger pots until they become unwieldy, and then, of course, they have to be divided.

Some plants habitually break many leads; others give rise to only one lead a year. Even plants that give many leads do not develop all the buds that are capable of producing new growths. Many buds remain dormant at the nodes of older parts of the rhizome. Removing the lead growth, as when a plant is divided, stimulates one or more buds on the older part to develop. Thus when a plant is cut in two, the younger part with the lead growth goes on as before, while the "back-bulbs" or older part, now deprived of a growing end, will develop new lead growths from dormant buds. There is sometimes a question as to whether to divide a plant with several leads, but there is no question when it comes to a one-lead plant of eight or nine pseudobulbs. If the latter is simply potted again, the chances are that it will go on giving only one lead, so that you get no increase in flower production for an ever larger pot. By dividing it you get two plants that will flower.

A lead division consisting of four or five strong pseudobulbs with leaves should flower on the first growth after division. A backbulb division of several pseudobulbs with leaves may flower on its first new growth, or may wait for the second year. But a weak backbulb division, one that has only one or two pseudobulbs, often without leaves, will make but a small growth its first year, one a little larger the second, and may wait for the third year to flower. For this reason, unless they are from a valuable plant, we ordinarily do not save the oldest pseudobulbs.

Since plants do not conform to any one pattern, little problems come up as to where to make a division. Try to make each division a strong plant. In dividing a one-lead plant, keep at least four pseudobulbs together for the front division, making the cut through the rhizome behind the fourth pseudobulb. Use your own judgment about saving the back part. In dividing a plant with many leads, it is not necessary to break it up completely into one-lead plants. Some leads may have developed so recently that to separate

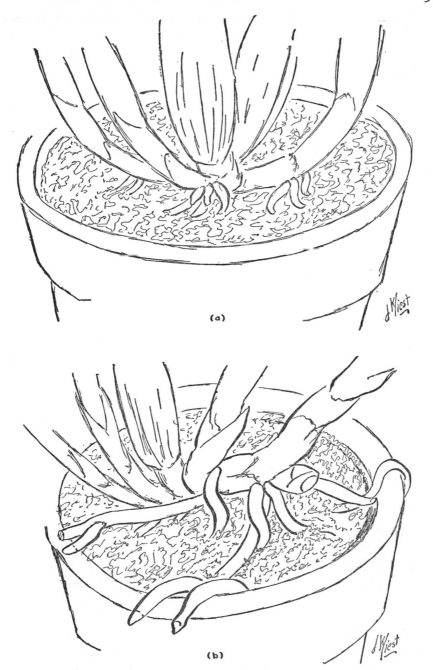

(a)

(b)

Fig. 9–5. A three-lead division (a) takes up about the same amount of space as a one-lead division (b).

them would make divisions of only two pseudobulbs. Rather, try to keep them in neat groups, perhaps two leads on one division, or even three, making the cut behind the pseudobulbs from which they arose so that they are joined as one plant. When repotting a plant that is not large enough to be divided, it may be wise to remove the oldest pseudobulb just to economize space. When a plant has recently matured from seedling stage, we often remove the small pseudobulbs remaining from this stage as they do not contribute much to the plant. Sometimes this enables you to put it back into the same size pot again.

POTTING EQUIPMENT

The equipment for potting is not fancy, but it is best to have what you need at hand before the plants reach a critical state. The various pieces of equipment and their use follow.

A potting stick. These can be bought from orchid dealers or can be made. One commercial type, of aluminum, has a large end and a small end, and another has a rubber grip for your hand. You can make your own out of hard wood, possibly an old axe handle. For large plants the blade should be about an inch and a half wide, rounded at one end to fit your hand, and thinned to a bevel at the other end. A small one can be made for seedlings and other small plants.

Osmunda fiber. Order a good quality of mixed grades. Use the coarser, heavier fiber for large plants, and the finer or softer pieces for seedlings. We like to pot with damp fiber as it is easier to work with and its pliability allows a firmer job. Before you actually remove a plant from its pot, prepare the new fiber by soaking and draining several large pieces.

A hatchet for chopping fiber. Some growers like to saw the fiber into slices while dry. We prefer to chop it while it is damp, chopping the pieces crosswise to give chunks of appropriate thickness for the purpose.

A heavy plank. A piece of 2 × 8 inch plank about two feet long makes a good chopping board for the fiber.

Stakes. Since the stakes stay in the pot with the plant for two or more years, they are best made of rustproof and decayproof material. You can buy galvanized stakes of various lengths. We have found that aluminum or steel clothesline makes good stakes, and we file off the desired length when needed.

String. For tying up the growths, florist's waxed linen thread is good, or some other soft but non-stretchable string. It should be thick enough not to cut into the tender growths.

Labels. Plastic labels that can be tied to the plant are good, the kind that can be written on smoothly and which does not allow the pencil marks to be rubbed off. It is surprising how easily a label stuck in a pot can be lost. Every plant should be labeled when it is potted.

Red clay pots of assorted sizes. We do not like glazed pots for orchids as they do not allow sufficient aeration. There is no reason why a clay pot cannot be set in a jardinière with space around it inside, however. Baskets of redwood or cypress may also be used and are pleasing to the eye. They are difficult to keep watered, because they dry out rapidly and water tends to run over the sides rather than to penetrate. We do not advise them for hanging in a window. Clay pots should have the hole enlarged to allow free aeration and drainage. Turn the pot upside down and break in the edges of the hole until it is about the size of a silver dollar. Pots with slits at the bottom may be used if you wish but are not necessary. We use pots of standard height for the most part, although we like three-quarter pots in large sizes and for community pots. Pots should be soaked in plain water before using, and old pots should be scrubbed clean.

POTTING

Choose a pot to allow space for two years' growth, estimated by the space between pseudobulbs. Set the plant to be potted in a bucket of water for ten minutes. This will usually loosen roots clinging to the pot so that it can be knocked out easily. If roots cling to the outside of the pot, clip them with scissors at the rim. Even though they could be pried away from the pot, they will not survive. Roots that have gone over the side and hang free should also be clipped, so that stubs about two inches long remain. To knock the plant out, hold it upside down and tap the rim on the bench.

Beginning at the back end of the plant, pull away the old fiber, especially the decomposed fiber in the core, loosening the roots as you go. Leave the fiber intact under the younger part of the plant to give a solid ball to which to pot. Trim off the portions of roots that dangle out of this ball, leaving clean stubs intact in the ball. There is no percentage in trying to save long root ends, as they will be broken in the potting process. Roots on the surface of the fiber should be trimmed to come to the edge of the ball. These and stubs of roots that had gone over the edge of the pot should be left on the

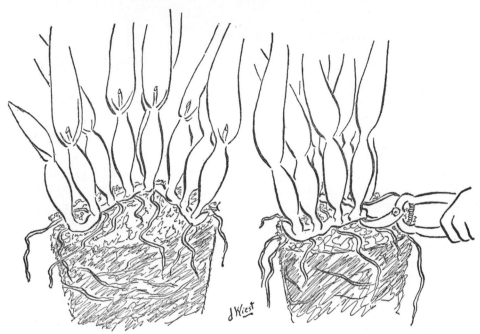

(a) This plant was a two-lead division when previously potted, and will now be made into two one-lead divisions.

(b) The rhizome is severed behind the fourth pseudobulb.

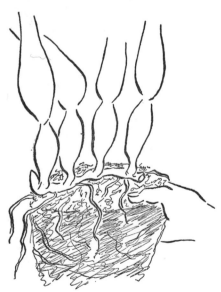

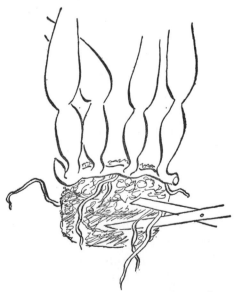

(c) After the parts are separated, the ball of fiber and roots will have to be trimmed down.

(d) Trimming off root ends to leave clean stubs intact in the ball of fiber.

FIG. 9–6. Dividing and potting a Cattleya.

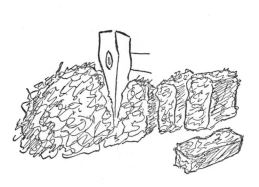

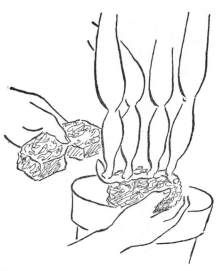

(e) Chop a large piece of fiber into chunks.

(f) Place a large chunk with a notch cut out under the lead. Fill in the back end with another chunk if it has an empty place.

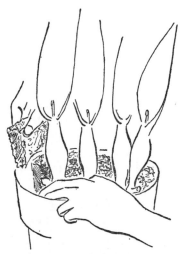

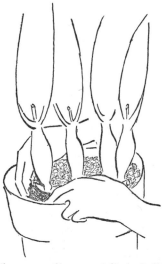

(g) Set the division in the pot, with the cut end close to the side of the pot. Stuff shredded pieces down around the ball in the bottom of the pot to hold the ball firmly, leaving two inches of space to the top. Now fill in around the ball with solid chunks, pressing the ball toward the back each time to make room for the next piece.

(h) The pot will seem full, but there is room for more fiber. Insert your fingers between the pot and fiber and press the whole mass back in the pot to prove this.

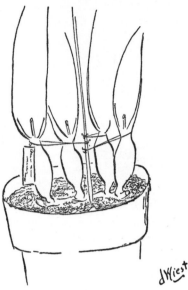

(i) Lay a chunk of fiber across the rim and catch it in the middle with the potting stick. Force the stick down and toward the center of the pot. This will force the chunk down between the pot and the rest of the fiber, straightening it in the process. Force in as many pieces as necessary to make the whole mass even and hard.

(j) Tie each pseudobulb to a stake, and label the plant.

surface as you pot the plant. All root stubs should give rise to many branch roots, which will renew the root system quickly.

Cut off and discard shriveled, leafless backbulbs. Pull away the dry tissue (old sheathing leaves) that has loosened from the pseudobulbs. Do not try to peel it off the rhizome as you may damage the dormant buds, nor from the younger growths. If this plant is not to be divided, it is now ready to go into its new pot.

If the plant is to be divided, study it as you start to remove the old fiber. When you reach the point where a group of older bulbs, backbulbs, can be removed, sever the rhizome and lay aside this part. Now make the front division, and ease apart the two halves of the plant. Leave each half with a good ball of fiber, and trim it up as described above.

Place several pieces of crock in the bottom of the pot to prevent the settling of the fiber over the hole. Use large pieces, to about one-fourth the depth of the pot. Shred a piece of fiber and lay it over the crock.

Take the plant, or division, in your hand. If the ball of fiber has an empty place in it, which is likely where you have removed the crumbly core fiber, fill this in with a solid chunk of fiber. Set the plant experimentally in the pot. The surface of the fiber, or the rhizome, should sit just level with the rim at this stage in the process and will be settled down to about half an inch below the rim. If the ball sits too high, remove a piece or two of crock; if too low, add a little more fiber over the crock.

Cut a large chunk of fiber with a notch in it and fit this under the lead, settling the plant back in the pot so that its back end is as close to the edge of the pot as possible. This is to give growing space to the front end. Now stuff chunks of fiber that have been loosened up a little down into the pot around the bottom of the ball to hold it firmly, leaving two inches to the top of the rim.

The next steps are a little tricky. Solid chunks of fiber are set into the pot, with the fiber grain as nearly vertical as possible, to fill in the space around the ball. Each time you put in a piece, keep the plant pressed toward the back of the pot. When the pieces are all in place, the pot will appear full, but there is still room for another series of chunks all around. Insert your fingers in front of the lead end, between the pot and the fiber, and press back the fiber and you will see that this is true. The next pieces will have to be forced in with a potting stick. Lay a chunk of fiber on its side across the rim, and catch it in the middle with the end of the potting stick. Force the potting stick down and toward the center of the pot. This will force the chunk of fiber between the pot and that which is already in place. The potting stick straightens out the chunk so that it slides in beside the rest of the fiber. It takes a strong arm! More pieces must be forced in until you absolutely cannot get your fingers down between pot and fiber, and the whole must have the firmness of hard sod. This is what we call potting "hard."

The fiber should be level across the top, and about a half inch below the rim. Any stray wisps sticking up can be trimmed off with scissors. Drive a stake into the fiber near the rhizome. If the fiber is firm enough this should require quite a little force. Tie each pseudobulb to the stake by itself. Wind the string once around the stake, then out and around the pseudobulb where it is joined by the leaf, and back to the stake where it is tied. Label the plant.

CARE AFTER POTTING

After being repotted, the plant should be given a little extra shade and its foliage should be syringed frequently. The roots will be inactive until new roots are formed and, during this period, cannot absorb water. Syringing the leaves and pseudobulbs enables the plant to replace water lost by evaporation. Do not give water in the pot until the new roots are two or three inches long. When you see the new root tips growing out, include them and the surface of the fiber in the syringing. We call this treatment keeping the plants "on the dry side." You will be well repaid for resisting the temptation to water too soon, for in these few weeks the old root stubs, which might rot away if the fiber were kept wet, will make a healthy new root system. When the plant is thus reestablished with enough root area to make use of full waterings, put the plant on a normal watering schedule and remove the extra shade.

POTTING BACKBULBS

If a set of backbulbs has a fair number of roots, treat it like a division as described previously. However, although orchid roots live for years if well cared for, the backbulbs sometimes have few or none left. Also, in breaking up a plant, sometimes there is not much fiber left under the back end. Thus there is little left to anchor the backbulbs in the pot. One handy method is to fasten a large, solid chunk of fiber under the rhizome by tying it firmly in several places with string. Then proceed as before. Another method, especially useful for backbulbs with no roots at all, is to fill the pot with fiber by setting in chunks side by side, as firmly as for other plants, and then to pry open a groove in the top in which the rhizome of the backbulbs is set. Bend a short length of wire into a staple and push this down into the fiber across the rhizome. Tie the pseudobulbs firmly to a stake. Often no new roots will form until the new growth makes its own. Therefore, syringe the backbulbs and the new growth frequently until the roots are well along.

AN ADDITIONAL TECHNIQUE

Occasionally a plant outgrows its pot before it has been in it long enough for the fiber to have broken down. This sometimes happens with a seedling or a division that breaks more leads than expected, or which may make two sets of growths in one year. It is not necessary to break up the fiber and trim the roots, but instead the plant may be simply shifted on into a larger pot. The plant is knocked out, set intact in its new pot, and chunks of fiber are forced in around the ball. It should be kept on the dry side for two or three weeks until it is obviously growing vigorously again.

CHAPTER X

CARE OF SEEDLINGS

T HERE is something about growing a plant all the way from an early stage that gives a special feeling of achievement. There is also an aura of mystery surrounding a seedling that increases as it approaches maturity, for not until it flowers will you know the secret it has held during its development. It is an experience everyone should have.

The earliest stages of seedling growth are easy to manage in the house, for they require a soft light and a warm, humid environment. Large numbers of young seedlings can be accommodated in a small space, so that if you plan to have a greenhouse within a year or so, you can get a head start by growing some seedlings indoors. By the time they are outgrowing a two-and-a-half-inch pot—in other words, by the time they are half grown—they will have the same light and temperature requirements as adult plants. Therefore, if a greenhouse is not in your future, or at least some expansion of growing space, it is not wise to acquire very many seedlings.

An orchid seed pod is started on its way by placing the pollinia from one flower on the stigma of another. The pod takes from six months to a year to ripen, depending on the kind. When the seed is ripe, the pod is harvested and the seed stored in a dry, cool place, often in a desiccator in a refrigerator. The seed is almost powdery, just discernible with the naked eye as small white or brown elongated particles. In nature the seed is windborne, wafted from the pod and scattered by air currents. Of the hundreds of thousands of seed in one pod, only a few will find just the right conditions for germination, such as a damp pocket of humus shaded by other plants. The tiny seed does not store much food, and so the developing seedling depends on fungi to release sugar and nutrients for its use.

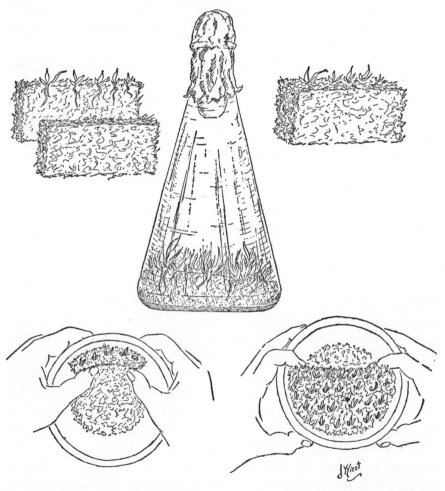

FIG. 10–1. Potting seedlings from flask to community pot. Center, a flask containing seedlings ready for transplanting. Upper left, seedlings are laid on a thin, neat slice of osmunda fiber. Upper right, another slice is laid over this. Lower left, the "sandwich" is set in the prepared pot. Lower right, many "sandwiches" of seedlings are set in the pot side by side. Each time, those already in the pot are gently pressed together to make room for the next one.

In cultivation sugar and nutrients must be provided for the use of the seedlings. Dr. Lewis Knudson of Cornell University, in 1922, developed the method of germinating the seed now in use. The seed is disinfected to kill any mold spores and is then sown in sterile flasks or bottles on an agar jelly containing the necessary mineral salts and sugar. After the seed is sown, the flasks are stoppered to prevent the entrance of mold spores, and the stopper is covered with foil or polyethylene film to protect it from contamination. The flask acts as a little greenhouse, in which the seedlings develop without disturbance or injury.*

The seedlings remain in the flasks for about a year, at which time they are ready to be transferred to pots.

COMMUNITY POTS

When the seedlings are about half an inch tall (some kinds become larger in the flask), they are transferred to osmunda fiber in community pots. Some growers put them in flats, but we believe the three-inch or five-inch pots are better for the average amateur. Twenty to thirty plants can be put in one pot, the advantage of which is that they can be kept more uniformly watered than the tiny "thumb" pots once used.

In order to remove seedlings from the flask, a small amount of water at about 70°F is poured in and swirled around, and then water and seedlings are poured into a shallow bowl. Two or three repetitions should remove most of the plants. The last few which may be buried in the agar can be lifted out with a dinner knife. Any agar clinging to the roots will dissolve away in the water. The process of potting is shown in Figure 10-1.

Community pots require a humid atmosphere, a night temperature of 60° to 65°F, and should not be allowed to dry out. They can be put in an orchid case in which you are growing warm orchids (see Chapter VII), placed so that they are well shaded by other plants. Or they can be grown in a small case, if you have one, or a "growing box" made from a fruit lug with a glass lid. Community seedlings require about 200 foot-candles of light when they are just out of the flask (about the same light required for the flasks themselves), which can be increased in a month or two to 300 foot-candles, and in another month to 400 foot-candles. The growing box or seedling case may be set near a window, with appropriate shade, or in a greenhouse. Shade

* For details on growing and sowing seed and the care of the flasks, see *Home Orchid Growing*, by R. Northen, D. Van Nostrand Co., Inc., 1950.

can be provided by placing a piece of muslin or two or three thicknessess of cheesecloth over the glass lid.

The seedlings must have some ventilation, for even though they like a high humidity they cannot compete with molds and algae likely to grow under too damp conditions. The glass lid should be propped up a crack, or the top part of the front and back of the box should be lowered to allow air movement. A slight opening will allow exchange of air without lowering the humidity too much. We would rather have this ventilation and spray the plants once a day than to keep the air saturated.

FIG. 10–2. A growing box for small seedlings, made from a fruit lug with a piece of glass for a lid. A piece of muslin or cheesecloth is used for shading. Note that the front and back sides are lower than the ends, to give ventilation when the lid is down. These plants are just out of a community pot. The larger ones, and those that show a good new growth coming, have been put in individual pots, while the rest have been put back in communities.

The community pots should be watered often enough to keep the fiber damp, but in the humid atmosphere of the box or case, and with the daily syringing, they may not have to be watered very often.

The tiny seedlings are suspectible to damping off. To prevent this, water the pots when they are first planted with a solution of Wilson's Anti-Damp, made up according to directions, and repeat at two- to three-month intervals.

INDIVIDUAL POTS

The plants remain in community pots for about eight months. By that time you will notice that some have become quite sturdy plants, while others are still fairly small. The larger ones are ready for individual two-and-a-half-inch pots, while the smaller ones should spend a few more months in communities.

To prepare the plants for repotting, gently pry out the whole potful of fiber and seedlings, and then gently loosen it with the fingers. The plants are separated by easing each one out of the fiber, retaining a little fiber around its roots if possible. Some of the roots will be broken, but the plants will soon replace them.

Now take two small chunks of osmunda fiber, place one on each side of the roots, and gently force this as a whole into the small pot. A little practice will determine how much fiber to use to give it quite a firm consistency in the pot. The pots for these little plants need only a piece or two of crock in the bottom for drainage. The smaller plants may be fitted into new communities in the same manner, nestling each one in its fiber next to another until the pot is filled.

The individual pots should go into a growing box similiar to the one in which the communities stay, with the light intensity remaining at about 400 foot-candles for a few months and then increased to 500 foot-candles, or they may be put at the back of a warm orchid case. Night temperature is still kept between 60° and 65°F. As they become established and begin to make larger growth, ventilation can be increased, but they should still be kept damp in the pot.

After the seedlings have spent a year in these two-and-a-half-inch pots, they should have made a rapid increase in size. Cattleyas should make a pseudobulb and leaf three to four inches tall; Cymbidiums should reach five inches; Cypripediums should be two to three inches tall; Phalaenopsis leaves should be two inches long. This is the age at which we advise most beginners to obtain seedlings, for they are sturdy plants and have survived half of their life from seed to flowering size. Up to this point they have been grown alike, but from now on the light-demanding kinds must be separated from those that need less light. In the greenhouse, Cattleyas should be removed from the boxes and be put out on the bench in a spot only slightly more shaded than necessary for adult plants. They can take from 1000 to 1500 foot-candles, increased gradually, of course. Cymbidiums can be kept along with Cattleyas until they approach flowering size. They should still be kept damp in the pot and be frequently syringed.

Indoors, Cattleya seedlings of this age should have the same light given mature plants. If they are to grow in an orchid case or an enclosed window along with mature Cattleyas the humidity will be all right. On an open window sill, these small pots will dry out rapidly and must be watched carefully. Their foliage should be frequently dampened.

Phalaenopsis and Cypripedium seedlings of this age need a relative humidity of 50% to 60%, and light intensity still around 500 foot-candles. In a greenhouse they should be in an enclosure of their own or in a spot with sufficient shade and humidity. In an orchid case they may be placed so as to have more shade than mature plants.

Fertilizer is good for seedlings of all ages. The chemical fertilizers suggested for mature plants are suitable, given every two weeks in place of one of the waterings, or sprayed on the foliage.

READY TO FLOWER

When the seedlings outgrow their two-and-a-half-inch pots they should go into four-inch pots. An occasional very large seedling may merit a five-inch pot. This time they are potted as mature plants, for they should flower in these pots. The method of repotting is shown in Figure 10-3. It is not necessary to disturb the ball of fiber, as it is in potting a mature plant, and they may be moved whenever their growth merits it. After they have been repotted, do not water them for two weeks, but syringe the foliage daily. If potting is done in bright weather, give them a little extra shade until their roots are growing well.

The time required from flask to flowering size varies with the kind and with the speed of growth. Some plants are naturally more vigorous and make more rapid progress than others. If the average grower flowers Cattleyas in four or five years from the flask, he is doing a good job. Their growth can be speeded by the use of artificial light, as described in Chapter XII, but the average grower may not have the means or the inclination to do this. Plants grown indoors may take a little longer to reach flowering size because of the fewer number of hours of good light per day.

The first flowering of a seedling may be just as vigorous as that of a mature plant, but often the flowers are somewhat smaller and fewer in number than they will be the second time. Cattleyas sometimes make a sheath as they approach maturity but fail to flower in it. When this happens you can

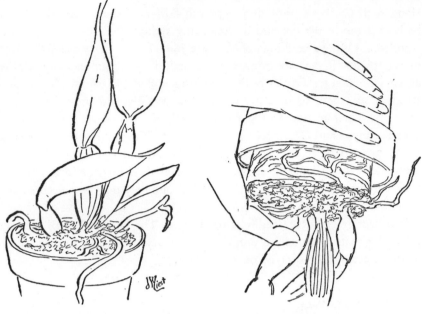

(a) The plant to be repotted.   (b) Knocking it out of the pot.

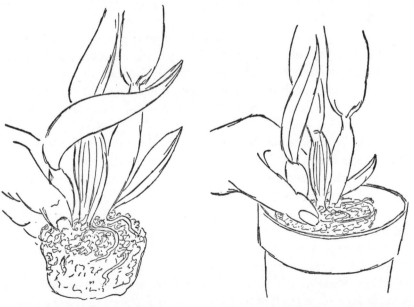

(c) The ball of fiber is left intact.   (d) Fitting it to its new pot.

FIG. 10–3. Moving a seedling on into a larger pot.

(e) Slightly shredded fiber is stuffed in around the ball.

(f) The fiber is worked down with a potting stick.

(g) More fiber is added if necessary, and all is worked down level to a good firm consistency.

(h) The finished job.

expect the next growth to flower. Phalaenopsis may produce only three or four flowers on their first spike, while the second may have many more. If the first flowers of a seedling are large and handsome, you can know you have a good plant. If they are small, yet of good color, shape, and substance, the chances are that they will be better the next time. If they are poorly shaped or colored, the chances are not so good that they will improve the next time, but it is worth waiting to see, for sometimes increase in size and vigor of the plant will produce larger heavier flowers.

CHAPTER XI

AILMENTS AND PROBLEMS

W HEN orchids are given healthy environmental conditions, few problems arise. Most orchids are quite tough and fairly resistant to diseases and the depredations of the usual pests. However, it is better to know what to look for than to be unprepared, and occasional ailments occur even in the best-managed collection. The following are the kinds of trouble generally experienced, although not necessarily of frequent occurrence, and their possible causes and prevention are described.

TEMPERATURE

If the rest of your plants flower, indicating that your general culture is good, but one or two fail, it may be that these particular ones are more sensitive than the others to night temperature. For instance, an intermediate kind may refuse to set flower buds unless it has a night temperature of 55° for two months or so after the growths have matured. You might try moving the plant to a spot with cooler night temperature. Some others may fail to flower if the night temperature is too cool. A little experimenting with individual plants that are temperamental may give results.

DAY LENGTH

Day length influences the initiation of flower buds in many plants, including some orchids, or it may control the development of the flower buds that have been initiated previously. In *Cattleya labiata,* for example, flower buds are actually formed by cells at the tip of the pseudobulb during the development of the pseudobulb in early summer. These minute buds are visible only with the aid of the microscope. They remain microscopic all during the summer and start to grow up in the sheath only as autumn comes on. The factor that brings on the growth of the flower buds is the short day length of autumn, and *C. labiata* is therefore known as a "short" day species. Growers who wish to have *C. labiata* in bloom for a certain date can control its flowering by giving it artificially long days until two months before flowers are desired. This is done by spacing 100-watt bulbs ten feet apart in the greenhouse and turning them on at sundown for as many hours as necessary to bring the total number of light hours to 16. Lighting must be begun well before the buds start pushing up in the sheath. As soon as the artificial lighting is discontinued, and the plants allowed to have the normally short days of fall or winter, the buds begin to grow, to open in about two months. This species has been held from flowering by long days for as long as a year. Many of its hybrids follow the same habit and are known as "controllable" hybrids.

Many kinds are prevented from initiating or developing flower buds by long days. On the other hand, some will do so only with long days. Each species has to be studied by itself, a long and tedious process, and, although much has been accomplished, we still do not know the habits of many kinds.

In a greenhouse, the day length follows the pattern of the seasons, but in a home the occupants make the days artificially long by the use of electric lights. Plants placed somewhat away from the light may not be affected, but those that stand near the lights may be prevented from flowering. It does not take a very high light intensity to make the difference between day and night for a plant. If some of your indoor plants fail to flower, it may be that they are "short day" plants. It would be worth experimenting with these by giving them short days as soon as the growth has matured. Perhaps you can move them into a room that is not used during the evening, or devise some other means of giving them ten hours of light and fourteen hours of darkness. We tried this on a hybrid that had not flowered in two series of sheaths. Two months after short-day treatment was begun, the plant was in flower on growths made both years. Once the buds are well up in the sheath a plant can be returned to the living room, for the long days will not cause the already growing buds to stop.

FAILURE TO FLOWER AND POOR FLOWER SUBSTANCE

Any environmental condition that impairs the health of a plant may be the cause of failure to flower, such as insufficient light, improper temperatures, or overwatering. A "blind" growth is one that does not flower. Failure of the growth to form a sheath may mean that it is not going to flower, but buds often come without a sheath.

When a sheath becomes dry, it may mean that flowers will not come. However, buds can come in a dry sheath, even as much as a year later. Do not cut off the dry sheath unless, when buds form, they seem to have difficulty pushing up in it. Then cut it off just above the tops of the buds. Sometimes in hybrids the sheath may be too small for the buds, or too long, or too tough. Sheath character is not always inherited to match the length of flower stem or size of buds. Keep an eye on the developing buds, and cut off the sheath's top or open it if the flower stems are becoming bent double in it or the flowers are too crowded. Some plants form a double sheath, which usually causes no trouble, but, again, if the buds have difficulty, open it.

Buds occasionally die in a normal sheath. We think the problem is a nutritional one in some cases. Either the plant is not strong enough to support the flowers, or some condition impairs the health of the plant while the buds are developing. Such conditions can be high temperatures (night or day), overwatering, or poor light. We have seen it happen with a seedling flowering for the first time, with a recently divided plant, with one heavily shaded by other plants, and with plants kept in an orchid case that is allowed to become too hot and steamy. Occasionally it happens on a plant flowering on many leads, where one lead may fail to develop its flowers.

Blasting of buds and flowers is a rare occurrence, but once in a while buds ready to open will turn pink or brown and fall off. They may have become too cold, for instance if they touch the cold window glass, or too hot if they have stood in direct sun. For a plant on a window sill, you might turn it so that the developing flowers are directed toward the room rather than toward the glass.

Poor substance—that is, flowers that are thin and fade before they should —may be an inherited fault or may be due to poor growing conditions. If a plant gives thin flowers year after year, failing to improve when culture is corrected, there is probably nothing to do but discard it. However, a plant that normally gives good substance may make thin flowers when some cultural condition is wrong. Our experience with indoor plants is that their flowers are of equal quality to those grown in a greenhouse.

SEPAL WILT

An ailment called "sepal wilt" or "dry sepals" occurs occasionally and is familiar to almost all Cattleya growers, for it seems to affect Cattleyas most widely. The bud develops until it is ready to open, and then the sepals are seen to be thin and dry, or of a leathery texture. The rest of the flower is normal, and the petals and lip last their usual length of time, but its beauty is spoiled by the thin sepals that soon dry up. In a rare few plants it may be an inherited characteristic. It may also be caused by poor culture, for we have seen plants improve with better culture even after having had dry sepals for a number of years.

The largest cause seems to be industrial gases in the air. It is also possible that the same injurious gases may be present in fumes from non-vented gas heaters. (Artificial gas is not recommended for heating greenhouses, unless the heater is separate from the greenhouse. Even with natural gas we advise having the heaters vented. There should be no harm to orchids grown in a home heated with artificial gas where no leak is present.) Some areas are badly affected when smog is present.

Sepal wilt can come on most unexpectedly. It shows up in opening flowers, not in those that have been open for some time. It may occur in two or three plants while others are perfectly normal, and it never seems to affect all of the plants. Sometimes a plant that has many leads may give normal flowers on those that flower first and dry sepals on the last to flower, or the situation may be the reverse. Such evidence seems to point to individual sensitivity of plants, as well as to a sensitive stage in the development of the flowers. If the flowers on the sensitive plant open before the causative condition occurs, the plant escapes injury. If the causative condition occurs before buds reach the vulnerable stage, or after they have passed the vulnerable stage, they are not affected.

Since the factor that causes dry sepals is transitory, and since it may have come and gone before the results show up, it is difficult to track down. Research has shown that ethylene gas will cause it. This is the chemical that is used to ripen fruit that has been picked green. It produces changes in Cattleya flowers equivalent to the aging process. When a normal flower becomes old, the sepals are the first to show the thin, dry texture. In a flower affected by sepal wilt, the sepals are the injured parts, making the flower appear old before it opens fully. Ethylene gas may be present in industrial gases, and it is also possible that other gases do the same thing. All we can do is first to try to control things that may affect the health of our plants, including venting the heaters, and then hope that no ill wind brings smog or wafts injurious gases our way.

FREAKS

Freaks can show up in any kind of plant, and orchids are not immune. A pseudobulb with a sheath and no leaf, a flower with no lip or with the wrong number of parts, a column fused to the lip, sepals fused together, petals that have some lip structure—any of these, or any other strange "mistakes" happen once in a while on perfectly normal plants. A freak flower can even occur on a stem with normal flowers. Some growers call such deformed flowers "cripples," while scientists call them "anomalies." They usually do not appear again on the same plant and are nothing to worry about. Nor are they of any value. Their cause is some accident in the development of a particular growth or a particular flower. It would require a deep-seated change in the genes of the plant itself (a mutation) in order for the freak to be repeated. An individual plant can have a quirk in its genetic makeup that causes crippled flowers to appear rather regularly, but such a plant may give normal flowers sometimes and deformed flowers at other times. Some of the yellow Cattleya hybrids are notorious for this. A plant that gives normal flowers more often than deformed ones may be worth keeping, but should never be used as a parent.

YELLOW LEAVES

If the leaves of a plant turn yellow, the first thing to look for is overwatering. The yellow leaves in this case are a symptom of starvation because waterlogged roots can absorb neither water nor minerals. Another cause may be too much light, which can destroy chlorophyll and bleach the leaves. A third cause may be cold, but in this case the leaves become rather mottled with yellow or yellow-green.

LIGHT BURN

A light burn is actually a heat effect. The tissues are killed by being raised to too high a temperature by light absorption. The burned area remains localized and eventually dries. If it occurs at the very tip of the leaf, it may be cut off after it has dried to improve the looks of the plant. If it is centrally located do not cut off the leaf, for any living parts of the leaf can still make food and contribute to the strength of the plant.

DISEASES

Diseases of plants are caused by viruses, bacteria, and fungi. As in any class of living things, some diseases are fatal, and some are not; some can be alleviated, and some, thus far, have no cure. Plants, like people, may show individual resistance to certain diseases, or some may be more susceptible.

Diseases caused by bacteria and fungi show up first as watery spots which become sunken and brown as the tissues in the area die. In contrast to a light burn, the spots usually enlarge or become more numerous. A disease may start at the tip of the leaf, gradually spreading down the length of the leaf. Or it may start in the rhizome, killing off pseudobulbs and leaves as it progresses. A few spots may appear and then became arrested if the plant is resistant or if its spread is controlled. Soft, succulent growth is more easily attacked than hard growth.

Bacteria multiply within the plant tissues and come to the surface in oozing droplets (often too small to be seen by the naked eye). Fungi send their cobweb-like body into the tissues, while reproductive spores develop on the surface. The diseases are spread by transfer of the droplets or spores to the surface of healthy plants. Insects, or human hands, or drops of water splashing from one plant to another can effect the transfer. If the surface on which the organisms land is wet, the bacteria multiply and the fungus spores germinate, to enter the leaf tissues by such openings as leaf pores, insect punctures, or wounds. *Water on the leaf or sheath or pseudobulb is a partner to the spread of disease.* Allowing the foliage to dry off after watering or syringing, and ventilating to assure an exchange of air and prevention of stagnation, are important steps in disease prevention. Sanitation, cleaning up fallen flowers and plant parts that can harbor disease organisms, and control of insects and weeds that harbor insects, are other preventive measures.

The use of a fungicide is a final preventive measure, although it may not be necessary if the foregoing precautions are taken. It is indicated if disease appears to have got a start among the plants. When this happens, first cease syringing and give good ventilation. Then spray with a good general fungicide, such as Fermate, an iron compound. Wilson's Anti-Damp, developed against the damping-off fungus, is also good. In an emergency, if neither is immediately obtainable, Bordeaux Mixture may be safely used. It is the oldest fungicide known and can usually be bought from dealers in farm and garden supplies. These fungicides lay a deposit on the plants that kills bacteria and fungi that spread to their surfaces. They will not kill organisms that have already entered the plant.

Surgery, cutting out the diseased areas, can cure a plant that has localized spots of diseased tissues. With a clean knife, cut out the brown part (even one or more growths including the rhizome, if necessary), making the cut well into the healthy part. Then dip the whole plant in a solution of Fermate or Anti-Damp, or smear the cut edges with a paste made of Bordeaux Mixture and water. Keep the plant dry for a week or two, and separate from other plants. It may be that the organism has already penetrated parts that look healthy, as in the case of a Pythium rot where the fungus is present in the rhizome and progressively kills off the growths. Removal of the dying parts in this instance cannot remove the cause. If, therefore, after removing diseased parts other parts continue to become diseased, it is better to discard the plant.

A sheath may turn black and watery, having been attacked by a disease organism. Sponge the sheath or dip the growth in a fungicide, and then cut off the sheath above the enclosed flower buds. Then dip the growth again so that the buds become washed in the fungicide. It may be that the buds have not been affected and can thus be saved. This condition is prevalent where the atmosphere is kept too damp.

In a stagnant, damp atmosphere, flowers may develop pink or brown spots, a blight that spreads quickly if affected flowers are allowed to remain in the presence of other flowers. Cut off all spotted flowers and destroy them.

Virus diseases are more elusive. They are treacherous because they cannot, at present, be cured, and because they affect the whole plant. All divisions of an infected plant will carry the disease. A virus is spread by cutting a healthy plant with shears or a knife used on a diseased plant, or by insects which transfer juice from one plant to another. Virus diseases may cause streaking of the leaves, fine yellow lines that become dark or black; or a spot that spreads in concentric rings, either round or diamond shape; or pitting on the underside of leaves with the darkened areas showing from the top surface; or "necrotic" areas, areas of dead tissue. One kind shows up in the flowers as a breaking or mottled affect in the color, with sometimes distortion of the flowers. All of these undermine the health of the plant, some to a greater degree than others.

Prevention of spread includes sanitation, control of insects, and the sterilization of tools used in cutting the plants. Tools may be dipped in 70% alcohol or in Clorox, one part in ten of water.

PEST CONTROL

Thrips, spider mites, aphids, and scale, along with slugs and snails, are the chief enemies of orchids at present. Growers used to fear the specific insect enemies that live with orchids in their native habitats, which used to come into this country with imported plants. The government inspection and fumigation service has forestalled further entrance of these pests, and modern insecticides have practically cleared them out of the greenhouses they had entered. The kinds that plague orchid plants now are mostly species native to the United States and which invade our gardens and house plants. During the summer one may find other pests than those mentioned, such as leaf hoppers, chewing beetles, centipedes, grasshoppers, etc., but these are not likely to come into the house.

Spider mites make minute punctures in the leaves and flowers. Their damage looks like gray stippling on the underside of leaves, and small punctures surrounded by a watery halo on flowers. Red spider makes a fuzzy web on the under side of leaves, in which the eggs are laid and the young hatch out. Some other mites do not spin a web. Thrips are small wingless insects and their damage is in the form of grayish or silvery scars on leaves and blossoms. Aphids are not common on orchids, but can be transferred to them from other plants. When any of these injure flower buds, the areas they damage do not develop properly and distorted flowers may result. Scale insects, which are free moving when first hatched, but which settle down in one spot and cover themselves with a hard shell, used to be common before the discovery of DDT, but are scarcely seen where DDT is used. They infest plant parts, often finding cover under the sheathing leaves that cover pseudobulbs and rhizome, and suck the plant juice.

DDT is effective against thrips, aphids, and scales, but not against the spider mites. Rotenone and Pyrethrum are somewhat effective against the mites. The Andrew Wilson Company, whose products we have described previously, make a spray called Super-Cide, containing 10% DDT plus Rotenone and Pyrethrum. It is a good all-around insecticide, especially made for use on orchids but good for all house plants. Regular use, every three or four months, should give good control of all four pests. Frequent syringing of the foliage also helps keep down the mites.

If the mites are not controlled by Super-Cide, products called Di-mite and Aramite (obtainable from dealers in orchid supplies) can be used, in greenhouse or orchid case. *The organic phosphates such as Parathion and Malathion are absolutely too poisonous to be used in the home,* although they are resorted to in greenhouses.

A pest that sometimes makes its appearance after its enemies have been destroyed by DDT is the common springtail, or Collembola. It is a small, slim, grayish, wingless insect that jumps when disturbed. It lives in soil all over the world, usually feeding on organic matter in the soil. They will attack tender root tips and, when present in large numbers, can do a good bit of damage. They can be controlled by Chlordane, used either as a spray or in dust form sprinkled in minute amounts on the fiber and watered in. One treatment is usually all that is necessary for a long time. It is better, however, to use it with extreme caution in very small amounts and repeat if necessary, than to use a large amount.

In the use of any insecticide, the directions and cautions given by the manufacturer should be followed exactly. Insects and plants are both made of living cells, and plants may be injured by substances that kill insects. Concentrations have been worked out that will kill the insects but not injure the plants, and so careful attention should be given to measuring the chemicals for spraying. Always use care to protect yourself from these poisons, too.

Slugs and snails may be partially controlled by hand picking, not too difficult a job when only a few plants are involved. Various slug and snail baits are on the market, containing metaldehyde as the active ingredient. Slugs damage new root tips and flower buds especially, but also attack young and tender growths. The most common snail seen is a small, brown, flat-coiled kind that seems to come in osmunda fiber. It can eat holes right through tender leaves.

CHAPTER XII

ARTIFICIAL LIGHT AND OUTDOOR GROWING

THE use of artificial light for growing African violets and for other plants of low light intensities has led to some trials with orchids. There is really little information as yet, for the attempts have been scattered and have been carried on under a variety of conditions and on different kinds of orchids. The positive results, however, give us a basis for believing that artificial light may be useful and practical in supplementing poor natural light and may even be used instead of daylight. Oddly enough, orchids under artificial light do not seem to need as high a total foot-candle intensity as they do with daylight. Ingenious placing of the lights and the use of reflecting surfaces can throw light on the lower parts and the underneath surfaces of leaves, which in nature or even in a greenhouse would be shaded by the upper parts of the plants. An intensity of 1000 foot-candles thrown on all parts of the plants can be made to do the work of 2000 foot-candles on the upper surfaces only. A bracket of lights placed over orchids in a case or on a window sill can help make up for poor light during dark weather or can give a few additional hours of light during the short days of winter. If any plants are short-day kinds (see Chapter 11), plan the hours of artificial light to coincide with the natural day length.

The lights must be close to the plants or else the benefit is lost, for the intensity of the light decreases rapidly as the distance from the source increases. Eighteen inches from the lights to the tops of the plants is a satisfactory distance to plan. A 15-watt fluorescent tube in a white reflector gives a reading of 2000 foot-candles exactly at the tube, a reading of 880 foot-candles with the light meter held one inch below the tube, and about 80 foot-candles twelve inches below the tube. Two 40-watt tubes in a white reflector give about 400 foot-candles at a level eight inches below the tube.

In order to make good root and top growth, plants require the blue and red portions of the spectrum, which can be supplied by a combination of fluorescent and incandescent light respectively. A proportion worked out for various kinds of plants, and which seems to give good results, is one 25-watt incandescent bulb to one 40-watt fluorescent tube. There is a small amount of heat from fluorescent tubes, but a considerable amount from incandescent bulbs, and this last should be considered in planning the use of lights. For instance, if plants are to be grown entirely by artificial light, the battery of bulbs may produce more heat than is good for the plants and a circulating fan may be necessary to keep the warm air moving away from the plants. Even one or two incandescent bulbs in an orchid case can heat the case and can be especially bad for plants located close to the lights, so that ventilation must be planned accordingly.

As to the number of tubes to be used, and the number of foot-candles necessary, we do not have sufficient data to make exact recommendations. Space is a limiting factor, for fixtures can be set only just so close together. Two or three tubes and an incandescent bulb in an orchid case would boost the light intensity for the plants in dark weather enough to be most helpful. Similarly, lights arranged to shine on the back side of plants in the window will furnish light to leaves and pseudobulbs normally poorly lighted. In dark weather, when perhaps only 100 to 300 foot-candles reaches the plants from the window, artificial light can nearly double that. Tubes and bulbs added to an orchid case do not detract from its beauty, but the utilitarian appearance of a bracket of lights in a window will detract from the charm of the window.

Cypripediums and Miltonias, which require around 600 to 800 foot-candles of sunlight in the summer and 800 to 1000 in the winter, have been grown and flowered by different growers at values between 200 and 750 foot-candles. The report at the lower intensity was for one season only, and the plants were perhaps coasting along on food stored up previously. Experiments at the higher level have produced fairly consistent results over longer periods. Seedlings of all kinds of orchids grown in daylight can be made to grow and develop at a faster rate by giving them extra light-hours by means of artificial light. For the hours over and above the normal day length a relatively low intensity seems to work, about 40 to 50 foot-candles, with the lights turned on at sundown and kept on to bring the day length to sixteen hours. The temperature during the lighted hours should be 68° to 70°F. As the plants approach flowering size, they should be given normal day length, in the event long days should prevent their flowering.

For plants to be grown entirely, or almost entirely, with artificial light, more tubes and bulbs must be used than where artificial light supplements sunlight. The basement set up shown here was devised by a grower in Detroit, where the dark winter days discouraged both growth and flowering. The wooden benches hold vermiculite, which is kept damp. Over this is a

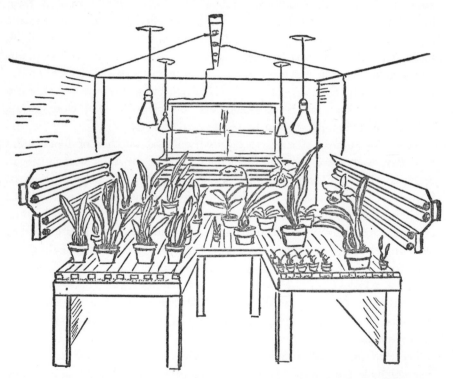

FIG. 12–1. A plan for growing orchids with artificial light in the basement. Reflectors hold four long Sylvania 4500 Å fluorescent tubes, to light the broad sides of the leaves. Overhead are four 150-watt, wide-beam, coated floodlamps. A reflecting screen (not shown) stands at the fourth side. (*Courtesy of George S. Fisher, M.D., Detroit.*)

platform of wood strips and hardware cloth on which the plants stand. The plants thus have air circulating between them and the vermiculite. The basement window gives 50 foot-candles of indirect light. Three reflectors, each containing four long Sylvania 4500 Å fluorescent tubes, are arranged to light the plants from three sides. Four 150-watt, wide-beam, coated floodlamps shine directly down on the plants. A reflecting screen (not shown) stands at the fourth side. The total foot-candle intensity is 750 to 800 foot-candles at the top of the mature plants, 200 foot-candles for the seedlings. The lights are turned on and off by a time switch, set to follow the normal day length of the season. When heat is needed it is supplied by an electric heater controlled by a thermostat.

Results under these conditions have been satsifactory. Plants showed improvement over the growth they had made in orchid cases in upstairs windows. Cattleyas have flowered well, as have *Lycaste Deppei* and *Oncidium Cavendishianum*. Cypripedium seedlings showed definite improvement, the benefit probably being due to the cooler conditions in the basement during the summer months. This last gives a suggestion to those who might like to try such a setup for cool orchids of moderate light demands in regions where they are normally difficult to grow.

As a plant comes into flower it may have to be moved to prevent the flowers from being too close to the lights. Most plants in flower can be moved to a spot in the living room, to be returned to their growing place when flowering is finished.

PUTTING PLANTS OUTDOORS

During the heat of summer, many growers like to put their plants outdoors. In the shade of tall trees, or in a lath house, where they have free air circulation and the benefit of cooler nights plants may be better off than in a house that does not cool down at night or where they need such heavy shade from the hot sun that they do not get enough light. Cattleyas, Epidendrums, Oncidiums, Laelia, and in fact many others of the light-demanding intermediate and cool types can be moved to the yard. We do not suggest putting Phalaenopsis outdoors, and question whether it would be worth while for other humidity-loving kinds whose light demands are similar. But Vandas may greatly benefit from it. In the warm southern states where the winters are mild some kinds can be grown outdoors all year long. In Florida, yards are decorated with banks of Vandas and Epidendrums. In Southern California, where it is drier, the Cymbidium has become a garden plant. In some backyards it may be difficult to find a safe spot for orchids. They cannot be put out in full sun, nor should they be in dense shade. In an area subject to hail storms few spots are naturally protected enough.

Plants usually do not need to go outdoors from a greenhouse, except that you might like to experiment with Cymbidiums. It may be possible to give them the brighter light and cooler nights they like in this manner. Cymbidiums moved out of a greenhouse are not as tough as those grown outdoors all the time, so that they should be given some shade from the sun at noon and in the afternoon.

When potted plants are put outdoors for a few months, they should be raised off the ground because of the danger of having worms and beetles enter the pots.

Before putting plants in trees, study the shade situation. Find a spot where the shade from mid-morning through the afternoon gives about one-fourth of full sun, with the light well broken up. Light from the east can be allowed more freely, but should be broken by shade by mid-morning. It might be wise to put out only a plant or two the first summer, to see how they fare, and then compare the results with plants kept indoors. If you find it beneficial, put more plants out the next year. Pots can be hung to the branches by loops of wire, or can be set on temporary benches or stands under the trees.

If you do not have trees to protect plants, a lath shelter, or lath house, will serve the purpose. A strong framework of posts should be set in the ground. The roof frame can be either peaked or flat. Across the framework the lath is nailed horizontally, running north and south to allow a moving pattern of light to fall on the plants. The laths should be spaced so that there is the width of half a lath between the strips. This is an approximate distance, but the danger in having the strips closer together is that you may cut out too much light. It is better to tack up cheesecloth inside, under the roof and the west side possibly, to diffuse the light rather than to exclude more. It will not be as hot in the lath house as in a greenhouse because there is not the glass to hold in the heat.

Inside of the lath house we suggest building low benches of hardware cloth on a wood frame, set fairly close to the cool ground. The lath sides can extend to the ground, or possibly only to bench level to allow more air movement under the benches. If the lath is extended to the ground, it can be more widely spaced than above the benches.

It would be well to spray outdoor orchids with a general orchid insecticide every few weeks because of the greater danger from insects. Be careful when using a weed killer in the garden. For instance, 2,4-D is injurious to orchids, and others may be as well.

Watering of outdoor orchids has to be adjusted to the amount of rain, the relative humidity of the air, and the amount of wind. With the free air movement and drying breezes, they will dry out more rapidly than you might think. Check them frequently. It may be necessary to water some every day, such as Cymbidiums and Vandas, and if the latter are in baskets they may need a twice-daily drenching with the hose. A plant that has been thoroughly soaked by a long rain will probably be much more thoroughly wetted than it is likely to be with a hose and may not need water again for two or three days.

INDEX

*Bold face numbers indicate pages on which
illustrations appear.*

Ailments and problems, 103-111
American Orchid Society, Inc., 7
  A. O. S. Bulletin, 7
Anther, 6, 53
Anti-Damp, 109
Anomalies, 107
Aphids, 110
Aramite, 111
Artificial gas, 106
Artificial light, and growth of orchids,
  112-115, **114**

Backbulbs, 84, 90, 92
Bacterial diseases, 108
Basement, growing orchids in, **114**, 115
Baskets, growing orchids in, 69
Bird-beak orchid, 67
Blasting of flowers, 105
Blind growth, 105
Bordeaux Mixture, 109
Brassavola, 30
  culture of, 49
  species of, *B. Digbyana*, 49
    B. nodosa, 49
Brassocattleya, 30, 31, 32, 49
Brassolaeliocattleya, 30, 32
Brassosophrolaeliocattleya, 30
Breeding orchids, 26-32
Bulbophyllum, 67
Burning of leaves, 34, 108
Butterfly orchid, 47
Buying plants, 7, 28-29

Care after potting, 92
Cattleyas, 1, 3, 12, 17-32
  age and flowering of, 99
  artificial light for, 115
  bifoliate group of, 18-19
  culture of, 12, 33-44
  cutting flowers of, 22

day length and flowering of, 104-105
dividing plants, 83-86
feeding of, 44
flowers of, 4, 18-19, **19**
flowering times of, 18
greenhouse culture of, 43-44
growth and flowering cycle of, 20, 21,
  23-25
humidity and culture of, 37-38
hybrids of, 28, 31, 32
labiata group of, 18
light and growth of, 34-35
orchid case culture of, 38-43
other orchids to grow with, 45-58
outdoor culture of, 115
overwatering of, 37
potting of, 79-93, **88, 89, 90**
root development of, 23, **24, 80, 81, 82,**
  83
seedlings of, 98, 99
sepal wilt of, 106-107
species of, *C. bicolor*, **19**
  C. Bowringiana, 19, 20
  C. Dowiana, 18
  C. gigas, 18, 20, 24, 28
  C. granulosa, 19
  C. labiata, 17-18, 20, 24, **104**
  C. Mendelii, 18, 25
  C. Mossiae, 18, 20, 25, 28
  C. Percivaliana, 18
  C. Skinneri, 19, 25
  C. Trianaei, 18, 20, 24-25, 28
  C. Warscewiczii, 18
temperature and growth of, 35-36
time to pot, 79-83, **80, 81, 82, 83**
watering, 36-37, 42-43
window-sill culture of, 34-38
Case for orchid growing, 15, 33-34; see
  also Orchid case
Charcoal, and potting of Phalaenopsis, 64

118

Chlordane, 111
Chopping fiber, **89**
Cirrhopetalum, 67
Cold orchids, 72
Collembola, 111
Column, 5-6, 53
Community pot of seedlings, 29, **95**, 96-97
Controllable hybrids, 104
Cool orchids, 6, 14, 72-78
Crossing orchids, 26, 27, 30-32, 94
Cutting orchid flowers, 22
Cycnoches, 55-56, **56**
Cymbidiums, 3, 29, 44
    culture of, 75-78
    flowers of, 76, **77**
    outdoor culture of, 115-116
    seedlings of, 98
    structure of, 76-77, **77**
Cypripedium, 3, 10
    artificial light and growth of, 115
    culture of, 52-55, 66, 73
    flower structure of, 53, **54**
    for cool case, 73
    for intermediate case, 55
    for warm case, 66
    hybrids of, 55, 66
    light requirement for, 53, 113
    potting of, 55
    seedlings of, 98, 99
    species of, *Cyp. Argus,* 55
        Cyp. callosum, 55, 66
        Cyp. insigne, 53, **54,** 73
        Cyp. Lawrenceanum, 55, 66
        Cyp. niveum, 55
        Cyp. villosum, 55

Damping-off, 97, 109
Dancing doll orchid, 49
Day length and flowering, 104-105
    and growth, 114
DDT, 110, 111
Dendrobium, 1, 44
    culture of, 64-66, 74-75
    species of, *D. densiflorum,* 75
        D. nobile, 74, 75
        D. Phalaenopsis, 64, **65,** 66
        D. Thyrsiflorum, 75
Di-mite, 111
Diseases of orchids, 97, 108-110
Distribution of orchids, 8
Dividing orchid plants, 55, 83-86, **85, 88,**
    90
Dry sepals, 106-107

Epidendrums, culture of, 45-47
    outdoor culture of, 115

species of, *E. atropurpureum,* 46, **47**
    E. cochleatum, 46
    E. difforme, 46, **48**
    E. fragrans, 46
    E. O'Brienianum, 46
    E. prismatocarpum, 46
    E. tampense, 47
Epiphyte, 9
Equipment for orchid grower, **43**
Ethylene gas, 106-107
Evolution of orchids, 4

Feeding orchids, 44, 64, 66, 74, 99
Fermate, 109
Fertilizing orchids, see Feeding
Fisher, George S., 114
Flask of seedlings, 29, **95,** 96
Flower buds, development of, **21, 22**
    dying of, 105
Flowering, 15, **21,** 22
    control of, 104
    day length and, 104-105
    failure of, 105
    of seedlings, 99, 102
    season for various Cattleyas, 18, 24-25
    temperature and, 14, 103
Flowers, see also kind in question
    basic structure of, 4-6, **4, 5**
    blasting of, 105
    desirable features of, 27, 28
    dislodgement of anther and flower life,
        56
    formation of, 104
    freaks, 107
    lasting of, 22
    poor substance of, 105-106
    prolonging life of, 43
    sepal wilt of, 106-107
    spotting of, 43, 109
    structure of Cypripedium, 53
    time to cut, 22
Fluorescent light, 113, **114,** 115
Fragrance, of Cattleya flowers, 22-23
Fungus diseases, 108
Fungicides, 108-109

Gases, injurious effects of, 106
Gaviota orchid fertilizer, 44, 64
Glass case, 15; see also orchid case
Greenhouse culture, of Cattleyas, 43-44
    of Cymbidiums, 75-78
    of Cypripediums, 53
    of Dendrobiums, 74
Growth and flowering cycle, 15-16
    of Cattleya, 20, **21,** 22, 23-25
    of Cymbidiums, 76, **77, 77**-78

of Dendrobium, 66
of Phalaenopsis, 63
Growth habits of orchids, 9-12, 13
Growth of orchids, as influenced by humidity, 15
  as influenced by light, 14-15
  as influenced by temperature, 14
  in baskets, 69
  on branches, 69, 70

Heating, an extended window, 40
  an orchid case, 41
Humidity, and growth of orchids, 15, 37-38
  in orchid case, 39, 42
Hybrids, 26-32
  choice of, Cattleya, 31-32
  intergeneric crosses, 30-32
  naming of, 28
  quality of, 28-29
  reason for making, 26, 27
  varietal names for, 29
  variety in offspring of, 27
Hyponex, 44

Incandescent light, 113
Indoor greenhouse; see orchid case
Insecticides, 111
Insect control, 110-111
Insects, and spread of diseases, 108
Intermediate orchids, 6, 14, 45-58

Knocking plant from pot, 100
Knudson, Lewis, 96

Labellum; see Lip
Labels, 87
Labiata group of Cattleyas, 18
Ladyslipper orchid, 3, 52
Laelia, 11, 30
  culture of, 49
  outdoor culture of, 115
  species of, L. anceps, 47
    L. autumnalis, 47
    L. flava, 49
    L. tenebrosa, 49
Laeliocattleya, 30, 31, 32, 49
Lath house, 115, 116
Lead, 20, 21, 22, 84
Leaves, light burn of, 34, 108
  yellowing of, 107
Light, 6, 113; see also plant in question
  and growth and flowering, 14-15
  and growth of Cattleyas, 34-35
  and leaf burn, 34, 108

artificial, and growth of orchids, 112-115
  color of, and growth, 113
  for seedlings, 96, 98, 99
  in an orchid case, 40-41
  day length and flowering, 104-105
Light intensity, from fluorescent tubes, 113
Lighting, to control flowering, 104
Lip, 4, 4-5, 53, 54

Malathion, 111
Maxillaria, 1
Metaldehyde, 111
Miltonias, culture of, 73-74
  light requirement for, 113
  species of, M. Roezlii, 74
    M. spectabilis, 74
    M. vexillaria, 74
Mites, 110, 111
Monopodial growth, 10, 12, 13, 57, 62
Mutation, 107

Naming hybrids, 28-29
Natural gas, 106
Nutrient medium for germinating seed, 96

Odontoglossums, culture of, 50-51, 75
  species of, O. bictoniense, 75
    O. citrosmum, 51
    O. crispum, 72
    O. grande, 50-51, 52
    O. pulchellum, 75
    O. Rossii, 75
    O. Schlieperianum, 51
Oncidiums, 1
  artificial light and growth of, 115
  culture of, 49-50
  for orchid case, 59, 60, 67
  growing on branch, 70
  outdoor culture of, 115
  root development of, 23, 24
  species of, O. ampliatum, 50
    O. cabagre, 50, 67
    O. Cavendishianum, 50
    O. flexuosum, 50
    O. Lanceanum, 50
    O. Obryzatum, 50, 51, 67
    O. ornithorhynchum, 50, 67
    O. sphacelatum, 50
    O. splendidum, 50
    O. varicosum, 49-50
Orchid case, 15
  and cool orchids, 72-73
  and culture of Cattleyas, 33-34, 38-43
  and culture of Cycnoches, 56
  and culture of Cypripediums, 53, 66
  and culture of Denbrobiums, 64

and culture of Epidendrums, 46
and culture of Oncidiums, 49-50, 67
and culture of Phalaenopsis, 61-64
and light exposure, 35
artificial lighting of, 112, 113
design of, 38-40, **59**
for locations other than home, 69, 71
growing seedlings, 96, 99
heating of, 41
humidity in, 42, 61
locations for, 61
miniature orchids for, 67-69
orchid tree for, 69, **70**
temperature of, 41-42
variety possible for, 1, 59, **60**
warm orchids for, 59-71
Orchid Digest, 7
Orchid Digest Corporation, 7
Orchid plants, structure of, 9-13
Orchid societies, 7
Osmunda fiber, 14, 44, 86
and use on slabs and branches, 50, 69, **70**
chopping of, 86, **89**
Osmundine, 14
Outdoor culture of orchids, 115-117
Ovary, 6
Overwatering, 37, 42, 107

Pansy orchid, 73
Paphiopedilum, 52-55; see also Cypripedium
Parathion, 111
Pest control, 110-111
Petals, 4-6
Phalaenopsis, 1
  and orchid case, 59, **60**
  culture of, 61-64
  fertilizing, 44
  growth habit of, 12, 63
  flowering of seedlings, 101
  flower of, **62**, 63
  hybrids, **62**, 63
  seedlings of, 98, 99
  species of, *P. Schilleriana*, 63
Pleurothallis, 1, 67
Pollen, 6, **53**
Pollinia, 6
Potinara, 30
Pots, 87
Potting media, 12, 14
Potting orchids, 79-101
  backbulbs, 92
  care after, 92, **97**
  equipment for, 86-87

mature plants, 79-93
seedlings, **95**, 98, 99, **100**, **101**
slab or branch, substitute for pots, 50, 69, **70**
stick, 43, 86, **90**, **101**
technique of, 87-91, **88**, **89**, **90**; see also specific kinds
time to pot, 79-83, **80**, **81**, **82**, **83**
Pseudobulb, 9, 10, 11, 18, **21**, **22**, 64, 76
Purchasing plants, 20, 28-29, 98
Pyrethrum, 110, 111
Pythium rot, 109

Red spider, 110
Repotting orchids; see potting orchids
Rest period, 15-16
Rhizome, 10, **11**, 20
  disease of, 109
  division of, **88**, 90
Root hairs, 23
Roots, 9-10, 11, 62
  branching of, 81, **82**, **83**
  development of, in Cattleyas, 23, **24**
  growth of, related to potting time, 79-83, **80**, **81**, **82**, **83**
Rotenone, 110, 111

Sander's List of Orchid Hybrids, 30
Sanitation, and disease control, 108
Scale insect, 110
Seed pod, 6, 94
Seedlings, buying, 29, 98
  care of, 94-102, **97**
  community pots of, 96-97
  first flowering of, 99
  flask of, **95**, 96
  growing in house, 94
  potting, **95**, 98, 99, **100**, **101**
Seeds, 94-95
  sowing in flasks, 96
Sepal wilt, 106-107
Shading plants, 34, 40, 41, 60, 76, 96, **97**
Sheath, **21**, 22, 105, 109
Short day species, 104
Sigmatostalix, 1
Slugs, 23, 110, 111
Smog, injurious effects of, 106, 107
Snails, 110, 111
Soil for orchids; see potting media and osmunda fiber
Sophrocattleya, 30
Sophrolaeliocattleya, 30
Sophronitis, 30
Sowing seeds, 96
Species, number of, 3
Spider mites, 110

Sprayer, **43**
Springtails, 111
Stakes, 86
Staking plants, **90**, 91, 92
Stanhopea, culture of, 55
  species of, *S. oculata,* 55
    S. tigrina, 55
    S. Wardii, 55
Stelis, 67, **68**
Sterilization of tools, 110
Stigma, 6
String, 86, 87
Super-Cide, 111
Swan orchid, 55, **56**
Sympodial growth, 10, **11, 64**
Syringing, 36, **43**, 92, 111

Temperature, and flowering, 14, 103; see
  also plant in question
  and growth, 12, 35-36, 41-42, 63-64, 66,
    72, 75, 98
  general groups and, 6
Terrestrial orchids, 9, 14
Thrips, 110
Tiger orchids, 50, **52**

Tools, sterilization of, 110
Two, 4-D, 117

Vanda, 12, **13, 57, 71**
  culture of, 57-58
  outdoor culture of, 115, 117
  Rothschildiana, 58
  species of, *V. caerulea,* 58
    V. Sanderiana, 57, 58
    V. teres, 58
Variety in orchids, 3
Velamen, 9-10, 23
Ventilation, 43, 97
  of orchid case, 38-40, 41, 42, 60
Virus diseases, 108, 109-110

Warm orchids, 6, 14, 59-71
Watering, 36-37, 42-43, 61, 64, 92, 97
  and incidence of disease, 108
  harmful effects of overwatering, 37
Wilson's Anti-Damp, 97, 109
Wilson's orchid fertilizer, 44, 64
Window, extension for growing orchids,
  39, 40
Window sill, artificial lighting of, 112, 113
  culture on, 1, **2**, 20, 34-38, 53